ALDEBURGH STUDIES IN MUSIC 5
General editor Jenny Doctor

BRITTEN AND AUDEN IN THE THIRTIES: The Year 1936

By the same author

BENJAMIN BRITTEN: A COMMENTARY ON HIS WORKS FROM A GROUP
OF SPECIALISTS
edited by Donald Mitchell and Hans Keller (1952)

THE LANGUAGE OF MODERN MUSIC (1963, 5th edition 1993)

BENJAMIN BRITTEN: PICTURES FROM A LIFE 1913-1976
compiled by Donald Mitchell and John Evans (1978)

MUSIC SURVEY, NEW SERIES 1949-1952
edited by Donald Mitchell and Hans Keller (1981)

BENJAMIN BRITTEN: DEATH IN VENICE
compiled and edited by Donald Mitchell (1987)

LETTERS FROM A LIFE: THE SELECTED LETTERS AND DIARIES OF
BENJAMIN BRITTEN Vols. 1 (1923-39) & 2 (1939-45)
edited by Donald Mitchell and Philip Reed (1991, 1998)

CRADLES OF THE NEW: WRITINGS ON MUSIC 1951-1991
selected by Christopher Palmer, edited by Mervyn Cooke (1995)

BRITTEN AND AUDEN IN THE THIRTIES: The Year 1936

The T.S. Eliot Memorial Lectures delivered at the
University of Kent at Canterbury in November 1979

by

DONALD MITCHELL

New edition
with a Foreword
by

ALAN HOLLINGHURST

THE BOYDELL PRESS

First published 1981
Faber & Faber
New edition 2000
The Boydell Press, Woodbridge

ISBN 0 85115 790 4

Aldeburgh Studies in Music
ISSN 0969-3548
Volume 5
Previously published volumes in this series
are available from Boydell & Brewer Limited

The Boydell Press is an imprint of Boydell & Brewer Ltd
PO Box 9, Woodbridge, Suffolk IP12 3DF, UK
and of Boydell & Brewer Inc.
PO Box 41026, Rochester, NY 14604-4126, USA
website: http://www.boydell.co.uk

A catalogue record for this book is available from the British Library

Library of Congress Catalog Card Number: 80-25980

This publication is printed on acid-free paper

Printed in Great Britain by
St Edmundsbury Press Limited, Bury St Edmunds, Suffolk

Contents

List of Illustrations
Foreword
Preface to the New Edition
Bibliography
Corrigenda
Preface (1981)   *page* 13
Acknowledgements   17

I.   Our Hunting Fathers   19
      Notes   50

II.   Sound-tracks   57
      Notes   94

III. Schoolroom and Cabaret   103
      Notes   125

IV.   On this Island   133
      Notes   160

      Index   171

Illustrations

Cover

Britten and Auden in New York (1941)

Within the text

1	Britten's diary: 1 January 1936	*page* 18
2	Manuscript sketch: 'Rats Away!'	40
	(*Our Hunting Fathers*)	
3	Britten's diary: 15 January 1936	56
4	Song sheet: *Pacifist March*	68-9
5	Manuscript: *Russian Funeral*	74-5
6	Manuscript: *Night Mail*	82
7	Britten's diary: 26 February 1937	102
8	Programme: *Up the garden path*	106
9	Manuscript: *F6* Blues	123
10	Britten's diary: 8 January 1937	132

Between pages 88 and 89

1	'Up in a balloon, boys!' Hedli Anderson performing one of her favourite music-hall songs (1930s)
2	A publicity photograph of Britten (late 1930s)
3	Auden, Stephen Spender and Christopher Isherwood on Rügen Island (1931)
4	Auden, William Coldstream and Britten posing as 'The Three Graces' at the Downs School, Colwall (June 1937)
5	Auden with Hedli Anderson and William Coldstream at the Downs School, Colwall (June 1937)
6	Isherwood and Auden in Central Park, New York (1938)

Foreword

W. H. Auden has long been seen as a defining figure of the literature of the 1930s: both its epitome and its shaping force. Donald Mitchell's book traces this influence in another sphere, through Auden's collaborations with the young Benjamin Britten. It is a study of a fertile artistic relationship as well as a revealing sketch of the shared milieux and media – cabaret, song, film, theatre – in which Britten learned his craft and tested his gift. Auden was a stimulus to Britten, an enabler, a darer who was also a dazzling technician; and it is fascinating to observe the younger man as he reacts to the challenge of Auden, intimidated by the poet's intellect but drawn to him by a shared alertness to the crises of the era, and exhilarated by the possibilities and demands of their shared projects. Though he would of course go on to greater mastery, range and depth in the years when his close friendship with Auden was over, Britten was surely never more brilliant or more happily suggestible than he was in the later 1930s and early 1940s. Auden had already synthesised an extra-ordinary personal rhetoric to address the problems and preoccupations of the age, and we can watch Britten too, through his twenties, exploring and absorbing the composers – Mahler, Berg, Stravinsky and Shostakovich among them – whose influence was to lend his music its new (and distinctly European) dimension. It is clearly more than coincidence that his Europe-consciousness was musical as well as political; he came to maturity as an artist in an unprecedentedly threatening and agitated age. One of the great resources of this book is the composer's detailed diaries, drawn on here for the first time; though Britten was not naturally a verbal person his recorded reactions to the darkening international scene have the clarity and urgency that are characteristic of his music at the time and thereafter.

It would be interesting to know in detail what Auden thought about Britten's later career (some of his known reactions are crudely disparaging). In his now famous letter written just before Britten and Peter Pears returned to England in the spring of 1942, he makes it clear that he thinks Britten in danger of settling down too soon, of settling into a role and a *modus vivendi* which will preclude his developing, personally and artistically, as Auden feels he should. There's a note of frustration to the letter, as if the promising pupil had not shaped up quite as the charismatic but slightly bullying master had hoped; and a typically dogmatic trick of objectifying the personal situation into an antithetical scheme, in this case one of Bohemianism vs Bourgeois Convention, of which Wagner and Richard Strauss are said to be the exemplars. Undoubtedly there are sharp perceptions in the letter, and they bear as much on Auden (he writes of 'middle-class Englishmen like you and me') as on his friend. But Auden was wrong if he supposed that Britten would turn into a Strauss – a bourgeois figure of huge technical accomplishment but reactionary in idiom and disengaged in subject-matter. He had underestimated the veins of anxiety, compassion and indignation which were to invigorate Britten's music till the end; and though the publicly political tone of some of the pre-war projects was never to be repeated, Auden should not perhaps have been surprised at the uncondescendingly democratic nature of much of Britten's later work for choirs, amateurs and children.

The fact is that Britten was an artist who after inevitable youthful rattling around took the earliest opportunity to live a life organised for his art, to know instinctively what it needed and didn't need, and to live and think and grow *in* his art. And as every page of his diary, and the scale and variety of his list of compositions, make clear, he was from the start a worker. His innate musicality and natural professionalism can be a frustrating mix for the kind of biographer or critic who seeks to explain away the music with ready or sensational patterns of psychological cause and artistic effect. Donald Mitchell, in his tireless and revelatory investigations of both Britten and Mahler, has always been properly sceptical of any facile pattern-making that does violence to the primacy and complexity of the musical works themselves. His endeavour, it seems to me, has been to present less the sustained biography of his composers (to every detail of whose lives he is none the less attentive) than the life-histories – emotional, intellectual, psychological and political – of the individual works of music they produced: their parentage, conception, birth, development, career and reputation. *Britten and Auden in the Thirties* is an exemplary contribution to our understanding of how one composer came to greatness, and what his greatness was made of.

Alan Hollinghurst

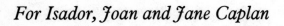

For Isador, Joan and Jane Caplan

Preface to New Edition

I have very little in fact to add to what Alan Hollinghurst writes in what for me is a strikingly perceptive Introduction, for which I am most grateful. In particular, I hope his cautionary words about the danger of 'facile pattern-making that does violence to the primacy and complexity of the musical works themselves' will be taken to heart. This is very much the current mode of biography and I am happy that Mr Hollinghurst shares my scepticism about it.

He mentions too, what I had begun to forget, that it was in these lectures that excerpts from Britten's personal diaries were made public for the first time; indeed, as I explain in my original Preface, it was my having access to the diaries that proved to be the *fons et origo* of the lectures themselves. Britten showed me these in the summer of 1976 – the year in which he was to die, in December – suggesting, with his customary diffidence, that I might find something in them of interest. I took them off with me to Bangkok – in the cardboard shoe-box in which Britten had kept them – and spent a long working vacation reading them and (for my own use) indexing them. I very soon came to realize how important a source they were, and how revealing and illuminating they were in regard to the Thirties and the youthful Britten's awareness of the troubled times in which he lived and when indeed he embarked on his career as a composer.

The need was to find a focus; and it seemed to me then, and still seems so now, that to concentrate on one critical year in the history of the twentieth century – 1936 – would precisely answer that need. One of the gratifying consequences of the years since these lectures were first published has been the attention paid to that remarkable Auden/Britten collaboration of 1936, *Our Hunting Fathers*, which has emerged from the virtual oblivion into which it was cast at – or rather by – the Norwich Triennial Music Festival of the same year. Britten's first cycle for voice and orchestra is now recognized as a major document of its time – Kurt Weill apart, who else was there in this period protesting on this scale and with comparable intensity at man's inhumanity to man? – and as one of the most arresting of Britten's early masterpieces.

The documentary films too in their own quieter way rightly continue to command attention and inquiry. Here, of course, Britten, along with Auden, was one of a team pursuing a ground-breaking medium. If this, the 'documentary', was primarily an *information* medium, Britten brought to it, as Philip Reed has most skilfully demonstrated, extraordinary qualities of both technical innovation and imagination. *Night Mail* (1936) has established itself as a *locus classicus*, on account of both Auden's marvellous text and Britten's invention of 'railway sound' almost indistinguishable from reality but in fact produced by an eccentric ensemble of 'instruments', including sandpaper and wind machine (see p. 83 for a more complete inventory). As for *Coal Face*, made in the year preceding *Night Mail*, it probably represents an integration of vision, sound and word (spoken and sung) that had not before been attempted in film. It was a moment in history, albeit one that went unrecognized by those creating or participating in it. (I cannot recall Britten showing even a passing interest in what must have been to him days and experiences beyond recall, though as I suggest here and there in my text, those experiences and experiments were to leave their mark – their fingerprint – on his music until the very end of his life.)

For the very reason that so much of the information given in the lectures was new – some of it, in fact, provided by some of Britten's Thirties associates still alive at the time, e.g. Paul Rotha – I decided not to attempt to re-write the text or expand it, thus diminishing perhaps the zest and sense of discovery and excitement that I had while putting the lectures together, and which I hope this new edition may retain. Errors of fact and transcription are dealt with in the Corrigenda list, which also includes the dates of those who have died since the book's publication. The addition of a select Bibliography I hope will prove useful to readers who may want to pursue their studies or, best of all, undertake studies of their own. There is much still to be explored and assessed, much still to be said.

The very last words with which this book ends read, 'We should remember them [Britten and Auden], and salute them, together'. At the time I did not myself remember to mention how, in 1973, when Britten was staying with us in Sussex, he responded to the unexpected news of Auden's death, 'with a storm of tears', as I was to write later. (It was the only time I ever witnessed Britten weeping.) I have no doubt that in those tears, grief and gratitude were present in equal measure.

Donald Mitchell
Chapel House
Horham

20-21 February 2000

Bibliography

Auden W.H., and Isherwood C.: *Plays and Other Dramatic Writings by W.H. Auden 1928-1938*, ed. Edward Mendelson (London: Faber and Faber, 1989)

Bucknell, Katherine and Jenkins, Nicholas (eds.): *'The Map of all my Youth': Early Works, Friends and Influences*, Auden Studies, vol. 1 (Oxford: Clarendon Press, 1990)

Carpenter, Humphrey: *W.H. Auden: A Biography* (London: George Allen & Unwin, 1981)

Carpenter, Humphrey: *Benjamin Britten: A Biography* (London: Faber and Faber, 1992)

Cunningham, Valentine: *British Writers of the Thirties* (Oxford: Oxford University Press, 1988)

Davenport-Hines, Richard: *Auden* (London: Heinemann, 1995)

Doherty, Barbara: "We know for Whom We Mourn': Britten, Auden and the Politics of 1936', *Tempo*, new ser., no. 192 (1995), 22-7

Hindley, Clifford: 'Britten, Auden and Johnny Inkslinger', *Perversions*, ii (1994), 42-56

Hynes, Samuel: *The Auden Generation: Literature and Politics in England in the 1930s* (London: Faber and Faber, 1979)

Kermode, Frank: *History and Value: the Clarendon Lectures and Northcliffe Lectures 1987* (Oxford: Clarendon Press, 1988)

Kildea, Paul: 'Britten, Auden and "Otherness"', *The Cambridge Companion to Benjamin Britten*, ed. Mervyn Cooke (Cambridge: Cambridge University Press, 1999), 36-53

Kovnatskya, Lyudmila: 'Russian Funeral through Russian Ears: Aural Impressions and Some Questions', *International Journal of Musicology*, Vol. 2 (1993), 321-333

Mann, William: 'The Incidental Music', in *Benjamin Britten: A commentary on his works by a group of specialists*, ed. Donald Mitchell and Hans Keller (London: Rockliff, 1952)

Mendelson, Edward: 'The Auden-Isherwood Collaboration', *Twentieth Century Literature*, 22/3 (1976), 277-285
___ *Early Auden* (London: Faber and Faber, 1981)
___ *Later Auden* (London: Faber and Faber, 1999)
___ 'The Making of Auden's Hymn for St Cecilia's Day', in *On Mahler and Britten: Essays in Honour of Donald Mitchell on His Seventieth Birthday*, ed. Philip Reed (Woodbridge: Boydell & Brewer, 1995), 186-192

Mitchell, Donald: 'Down There on a Visit: A Meeting with Christopher Isherwood', in *Cradles of the New: Writings on Music 1951-1991*, selected by Christopher Palmer and edited by Mervyn Cooke (London: Faber and Faber, 1995), 441-449
___ 'The Origins, Evolution and Metamorphoses of *Paul Bunyan*, Auden's and Britten's "American" Opera', in *W.H. Auden: Paul Bunyan: the Libretto of the Operetta by Benjamin Britten* (London, Faber and Faber, 1988), 83-148

Mitchell, Donald and Reed, Philip: '"For Hedli": Britten and Auden's Cabaret Songs', in *W.H. Auden, 'The Language of Learning and the Language of Love': Uncollected Writing, New Interpretations*, ed. Katherine Bucknell and Nicholas Jenkins, Auden Studies, vol. 2 (Oxford: Clarendon Press, 1994)

Mitchell, Donald and Reed, Philip (eds.): *Letters from a Life: The Selected Letters and Diaries of Benjamin Britten 1913-1976*, vol. 1: 1923-39, vol. 2: 1939-45 (London: Faber and Faber, 1991, 1998)

Northcott, Bayan: 'Notes on Auden', *Musical Times*, 134 (Jan. 1993), 6-8

Reed, Philip: 'Britten in the Cinema: *Coal Face*', in *The Cambridge Companion to Benjamin Britten*, ed. Mervyn Cooke (Cambridge: Cambridge University Press, 1999), 54-77
___ *The Incidental Music of Benjamin Britten: A Study and Catalogue Raisonné of His Music for Film, Theatre and Radio*, Ph.D. dissertation (University of East Anglia, 1987)

Seymour, Claire: *Britten and Auden 1935-1949* (MA thesis, University of Kent at Canterbury, 1993)

Sidnell, Michael J.: *Dances of Death: The Group Theatre of London in the Thirties* (London: Faber and Faber, 1984)

White, Eric Walter: 'A Bibliography of Benjamin Britten's Incidental Music', in *Benjamin Britten: A commentary on his works by a group of specialists*, ed. Donald Mitchell and Hans Keller (London: Rockliff, 1952)

Videos

Videos of the films *Coal Face* and *Night Mail* may be obtained from The Post Office Film and Video Library, Sittingbourne, Kent ME10 1NQ.

Select discography of *Cabaret Songs*

1. Sarah Walker (soprano); Roger Vignoles (piano) rec. 1982 Meridian (CD) CD-E-84167
Notes by Roger Vignoles

2. Jill Gomez (soprano); Martin Jones (piano) rec. 1992 Unicorn-Kanchana (CD) DKP(CD)9138 (producers: Christopher Palmer, Donald Mitchell)
Notes by Donald Mitchell

3. Della Jones (mezzo-soprano); Steuart Bedford (piano) rec. 1997
Collins Classics (CD) 14902
Notes by Philip Reed

4. Mary Carewe (chansonnière; Philip Mayers (piano) rec. 1998
ASV CD WHL 2124

Note: historic performances by Pears and Britten of *Our Hunting
Fathers* and *On this Island* were issued on CD in 1999
(BBC-B 8014-2 and BBC-B 8015-2).

Corrigenda

1. p. 13, l. 16 (and cf. p. 119, l. 29): for 'Speaight' read (recte) 'Speight'.
2. p. 17, ll. 26-27: Sophie Gyde died in 1983, Peter Pears in 1986, Beth Welford in 1989; see also references to Paul Rotha (p. 60, l. 4), died 1984, Christopher Isherwood (p. 96, l. 11), died 1986, and William Coldstream (p. 86, l. 21), died 1987. Other deaths include Alberto Cavalcanti (1982), Basil Wright (1987), Hedli Anderson (1990), Robert Medley (1994), and the dedicatees Isador Caplan (1995) and Joan Caplan (1997).
3. p. 19, l. 15: *Our Hunting Fathers* was in fact dedicated to Ralph Hawkes.
4. p. 28, l. 5: for 'G.P.O.' read 'T.P.O.' (i.e. Travelling Post Office, the alternative title of *Night Mail*).
5. p. 29, ll. 18 and 22: for 'G.P.O.' read 'T.P.O.'.
6. p. 32, l. 19: add 'ignorant,' after 'self-important,'.
7. p. 32, l. 20: for 'most difficult' read 'not difficult'.
8. p. 43, l.24: for 'minor ninth' read 'major ninth'.
9. p. 52, l. 16: for 'Dunkeley' read 'Dunkerley' (Britten's own mis-spelling has been retained in his diary entry quoted on p. 28).
10. p. 71, l. 2: for 'many fine things' read 'some fine things'.
11. p. 73, l. 33: for '£3000,000,000' read '£300,000,000'.
12. p. 80, l. 33: for 'G.P.O.' read 'T.P.O.'
13. p. 81, ll. 7, 14, 18, 23, 24: for 'G.P.O.' read 'T.P.O.'
14. p. 84, l. 5: for 'G.P.O.' read 'T.P.O.'
15. p. 84, l. 14: 'having to conduct' read 'having to conduct both'.
16. p. 84, l. 20: for 'thirty-three' read 'forty-three'.
17. p. 89, ll. 32-33: for 'the line from London to Southampton' read 'the line from London to Portsmouth'.
18. p. 105, l. 23: for 'this time' read 'again' (Auden had already taught at the Downs from 1933 to 1935, cf. n. 26 on p. 170).

19. p. 108, l. 4 (last word): for 'Field' read 'Feild' (Britten's own mis-spelling in his diary entry is retained).
20. p. 112, l. 2: for 'in the Cotswolds in 1936' read 'in the Malverns in 1937'.
21. p. 129, l. 32: for '7 March 1937' read '10 March 1937'.
22. p. 140, l. 1: but see DM's interview with Stephen Spender on 27 October 1990, cited by Humphrey Carpenter in *Benjamin Britten: A Biography* (1992), p. 327.
23. p. 157, l. 4: but see also n. 2 on p. 160.
24. p. 159, last line: for 'August 1976' read 'July 1976'.
25. p. 160, l. 21: Auden had first moved to Ann Arbor in September 1941; he moved house within Ann Arbor in January 1942 (see p. 161, l. 2).
26. p. 160, ll. 28-30: *A Shepherd's Carol*, also from *For the Time Being*, was broadcast on 21 December 1944.
27. p. 166, l. 2 (et seq.): *King Arthur*, Suite for Orchestra, arranged by Paul Hindmarsh, was published by Oxford University Press in 1996.
28. p. 173, column 2, l. 9: for 'Dunkeley' read 'Dunkerley'.

Acknowledgement
The 'programme as broadcast' billing for *Up the garden path* (p. 106) is reproduced by kind permission from the BBC Written Archives Centre, Caversham Park, Reading RG4 8TZ

Preface

Without the diaries Britten kept from 1928 to 1938, the Eliot Lectures for 1979 would have taken a very different shape. Because of the diaries, the composer is able to speak for himself, and I have not been sparing in my use of so basic a documentary source. I am grateful to my co-Executors of the Britten Estate for allowing me freedom to quote extensively from the diaries and for permission to use other source materials, both musical and literary. I have only minimally edited the quotations. Britten's spelling has been silently corrected except where a mis-spelling seems to make a point in its own right. His personal idiosyncrasies, e.g. the regular use of the ampersand, have been preserved.

I was happy, when scrutinizing the diaries, to come across this fragmentary entry for 5 January 1936 (a portion of the page, alas, has been torn out):

> Listen to a fine broadcast of T. S. Eliot's [*Murder in the Cathedral*] in which Robert Speaight . . . chorus of women are most . . . this is a fine play . . . & moving poetry. . . .

That Britten turned to the setting of poems by T. S. Eliot in his later and last years is common knowledge; but here was evidence of an immediate and admiring response from Britten's early years. Perhaps less well-known is the fact that after Britten's heart surgery in 1973, one of the few poets he was able to read was Eliot, in whose work he found certainty, strength and fortitude. Thus Britten's positive feeling for Eliot's poetry was of long standing. It was entirely typical of him that so many years passed before he actually set any of Eliot's verse: not until 1971, when in January he completed his *Canticle IV: Journey of the Magi*. It was a poem he had long had in mind but he did not attempt the setting until he felt himself ready to take on the challenge that Eliot's language represented.

I have no doubt at all that it would have given Britten particular pleasure to know that these lectures on his music in the thirties and his collaboration with W. H. Auden were to form part of a series dedicated to the annual honouring of a great poet's name. I was naturally conscious of the honour done me by asking me to deliver them, and I am glad to take this opportunity of expressing my warm thanks to the Master of Eliot College and the members of the Eliot Memorial Lectures Committee, not only for the invitation but for the generous welcome and hospitality offered me during the few days I spent on campus at the University of Kent at Canterbury in November 1979.

I must confess that I was somewhat daunted by recalling that it was Auden himself who was the first Eliot Lecturer; and I was further conscious of the fact that perhaps the topic itself — the thirties — would not have been much to his liking. However, as I remarked at the opening session, I had to hope for Auden's indulgence—or that he was engaged elsewhere on the evening in question: perhaps giving a lecture himself?

It is clear from my text, I think — though I would never have wished to conceal it in any way — that my account of the Britten–Auden relationship is necessarily seen through Britten's eyes and, more importantly, heard through the filter of his music. In the first stage of my investigation into 1936 I immersed myself in the music and was glad to find later that the intuitive deductions and interpretations I arrived at through my experience of it were confirmed by other forms of documentation and evidence.

However, although a certain element of one-sidedness undoubtedly remains, I — and my text — have greatly benefited from access to the typescript of Edward Mendelson's brilliant study, *Early Auden*, which will be published only shortly after this book appears. Professor Mendelson has most kindly not only allowed me to read his typescript but allowed me to quote from it in advance of its publication. I am much indebted to him and his publishers (in the UK, Faber & Faber; in the USA, The Viking Press) for this unusual gesture of friendly scholarship which, I believe, supplies a fresh dimension to my text. It does something to redress the balance as well as proving a source of further illumination and clarification.

Two final points. First, although it was never my fortune to meet Auden, I felt on finishing this particular piece of work that I had come to know him; and what I had come to know gained not just my admiration (Auden's work had had that from me already, for many years) but a whole-hearted affection and respect. He must have been a marvellous presence, though on occasion he could also appear to his friends in the role of a self-appointed (albeit affectionate) prosecutor: witness the remarkable letter he addressed to Britten in 1942 and here published for the first time (see pp. 161–2).

Second, although in Peter Pears's wise words, 'the later meetings [between Britten and Auden] were uneasy. The relationship had changed. . . .', he does not fail to remind us that Britten remained 'full of admiration and gratitude for the earlier years'. It was those feelings that were uppermost, conspicuously so, when Britten —then striving to recover from his operation—heard of the memorial service for his old friend on 27 October 1973 in Christ Church, Oxford, at which the *Hymn to St Cecilia* had been performed. It was only then, I believe, that Auden's death suddenly became real to him. It seemed to me that the years of unease were erased, at least momentarily; that gratitude and affection surged back and accompanying them a very sharp sense that the loss was 'major / And final, final'.

My formal acknowledgements I make elsewhere. Here I have to thank those without whose skills and help the lectures would never have been given. My thanks must go first to Jill Burrows, who did so much to quarry the lectures out of a vast mass of material and also prepared them for publication in book form. Next I must thank Kathleen, my wife, who produced many useful suggestions for shaping the lectures and was a constant source of encouragement and good advice. John Evans was my invaluable assistant at the lectures themselves, which involved no small amount of technology. That everything ran so smoothly was due largely to him.

Rosamund Strode, of the Britten-Pears Library, has been patient in answering my endless queries far beyond the call of duty or indeed friendship. The present text owes much to her unrivalled knowledge of the archive at Aldeburgh. Finally a special word of thanks to Paul Rotha, who helped to make possible the use of excerpts from two of his films, *Peace of Britain* and *The Way to the Sea*, thus completing the trinity of media—sound, word and sight — through which my collaborators and I attempted to explore the year 1936, and to all of which spheres our composer and poet might be thought to have made pioneering and influential contributions to the making of the thirties.

London, April 1980   D. M.

Acknowledgements

I am much indebted to Richard Alston without whose dedicated editorial assistance I should have found it difficult to see this revised edition through the press. I am most grateful too to my friends and colleagues at The Britten–Pears Library, Jenny Doctor, Keiron Cooke and Paul Kildea, for their sustained interest in the project and for their help, especially in compiling the Bibliography and a new set of illustrations and in correcting the excerpts from Britten's diary entries. My thanks also to Jill Burrows and Philip Reed for remembering after the passage of many years errors requiring amendment, and to Peter Righton for correcting proofs. Finally, thanks to Bruce Phillips, who gave early encouragement, and to Richard Barber both for his patience and impatience to have the book back in print.

JANUARY, 1936.

Wednesday 1

1936 finds me infinitely better off in all ways than did the beginning of 1935; it finds me earning my living – with occasionally something to spare – at the G.P.O. film Unit under John Grierson & Cavalcanti, writing music & supervising sounds for films (this one T.P.O. Night Mail) at the rate of £5, but owing to the fact I can claim no performing rights (it being Crown property), with the possibility of it being increased to £10 or £2 per day; writing very little, but with the possibility & ideas for writing a lot of original music, as I am going under an agreement with Boosey & Hawkes for a £3 a week guarantee of royalties; having a lot of success but not a staggering amount of performances, the reputation (even for bad) growing steadily; having a bad inferiority complex in company of brains like Basil Wright, Wystan Auden & William Coldstream; being fortunate in friends like Mr Frank Bridge, Henry Boys, Basil Reeve (& young Piers Dunkerley – tell it not in Gath) and afar off Francis Barton; being comfortably settled in a pleasant, tho' cold, flat in West Hampstead with Beth, with whom I get on very well; doing much housework but with prospect of having a woman in more than twice a week in evenings & once in mornings. So for 1936.

I. Our Hunting Fathers: Abroad and at Home

When looking at Benjamin Britten's development as a composer in the thirties, it seems appropriate on two grounds to select the year 1936 for special study, for intensive investigation. First, there is no doubt that 1936 was a key year, historically and politically; and politics was certainly one of Britten's preoccupations at that time. Second, 1936 was a key year for Britten himself as a young creator of phenomenal brilliance and originality, with a seemingly insatiable appetite for work; a year in which he himself felt that he had written his 'real' Op. 1. This was *Our Hunting Fathers*, the big symphonic song-cycle for high voice and orchestra that he devised with W. H. Auden during the year and which was given its first performance at the Norfolk and Norwich Triennial Musical Festival on 25 September. Britten himself conducted the London Philharmonic Orchestra and the soloist was the soprano Sophie Wyss, to whom the work was dedicated. It was performed again in a BBC concert of contemporary music a few months later, on 30 April 1937, under Adrian Boult (again with Sophie Wyss), an occasion that prompted Britten to remark in his diary:

> BBC Contemporary concert . . . cond. by Boult — BBC orch. They do my Hunting Fathers very creditably—I am awfully pleased with it too, I'm afraid. Some things don't satisfy me at the moment—but it's my Op. 1 alright. *

It is clear that already Britten was developing a capacity to discriminate among his own achievements and surely he was absol-

*This, and all subsequent quotations of a like kind, are made from the personal diaries that Britten kept on a daily basis from January 1928—the School Boy's Pocket Diary which he used for that year is inscribed 'Ben from Auntie Nellie'— until Wednesday, 15 June 1938. I am most grateful to my Co-Executors of the Britten Estate for allowing me to use the diaries, which are © The Britten Estate and not to be reproduced without written permission.

utely right to assess *Our Hunting Fathers* so positively. In this cycle the young composer stretched his creative powers to ·their maximum and perhaps flexed his muscles a bit too. He had every reason to be pleased with the results. The demands he made on his resources were richly met and, as I hope to show, brilliantly fulfilled.

A key year: a key work. *Our Hunting Fathers* is a work that one might say was peculiarly *of* and *for* its time, and importantly so. I am of course aware that I am in danger of falling into the trap that Samuel Hynes points out in *The Auden Generation*,[1] that is, of adopting the 'completed view' that emerges from writing— evaluating, assessing — after the event. A useful reminder, because in Britten's case the 'completed view' would give us a remarkably incomplete view of the music he produced in the thirties, and in particular of a work like *Our Hunting Fathers*. It is not just the simple case of a 'topical' work transcending its time; that would be far too glib an explanation. Perhaps one gets nearer to the heart of a complex matter if one poses a question, a riddle: was, say, *Our Hunting Fathers* made by the thirties or were the thirties made by it and its creators, Britten and Auden?

In attempting to answer that question one becomes acutely aware of a central paradox, a paradox that was perhaps a built-in feature of the art of the period. On the one hand, Britten's music from the thirties often appears to reflect the times, to be inextricably involved in, to be part of, the decade. On the other—and often precisely in those pieces which, like *Our Hunting Fathers*, can be too readily ascribed to the spirit of the thirties, to the prevailing *Zeitgeist*—the music represents both an emphatically personal view of the world and the manifestation of a quite distinctly personal creative voice; and, in the case of this song-cycle, something else as well: a major advance by the composer in the acquisition of vocal and orchestral techniques.

It is easy, too easy, and in my view wholly misleading to regard the thirties as a self-contained, closed period. It certainly had its distinguishing features, but one must, at least in relation to the accomplishments of the artists themselves, see it as only *part* of the

history of themselves and their various arts. Auden and Britten —
to name only two major creators — may have been decisive figures
who helped shape the thirties, but they were not exclusively *of* the
period: they developed during it, made their contribution, and
have an immensely long history of achievement *after* the thirties, a
fact that inevitably colours the way we look at their thirties pro-
ductivity. The period itself makes much more sense—and I
believe this also to be much nearer to a possible historical 'truth'—
if it is regarded not as a period with a defined beginning and end,
generating a kind of art that was peculiar to the decade but later
jettisoned or abandoned by its proponents, but as a stretch of time,
singled out by momentous historical events, preoccupied with a
certain category of ideas (some overtly political, some less so) and
with the media and techniques by which these might be best
expressed and, above all, fertilized by a group of artists, some of
whom brought to the decade concepts, passions and sympathies,
innovations and enthusiasms that were already established as
significant and powerful aspects of their personalities as creators.

Thus it is absolutely necessary to see the thirties, for Britten, as
an integral part of the *continuous* history of his growth as a
composer, albeit a highly important part. If one can understand
that the contribution he made to the decade was the result of being
the personality that he already was, and also, and no less interestingly, that his post-thirties development shows an equivalent
consistency, one is well on the way to comprehending the overall
consistency of his life's work.

I am aware, of course, that many of those active in the thirties
declared themselves in later years to be wholly disillusioned. But I
wonder if the period, on a slightly longer term view, was quite the
total failure that Auden, for example, thought it was, in his poem
'September 1, 1939':

> I sit in one of the dives
> On Fifty-Second Street
> Uncertain and afraid
> As the clever hopes expire
> Of a low dishonest decade. . . .[2]

Perhaps that — 'a low dishonest decade' — is how Auden felt things to be at that particular moment in history (and in his personal-life). Certainly it was a resonant date. But I think it could be argued that although the actual onset of war in 1939 must have appeared to those engaged in the political struggles of the thirties to be an annihilating blow that destroyed everything they had hoped and worked for, very many thirties ideals were achieved in the post-1945 era, especially in the legislation of the first Labour administration under Clement Attlee. I think it is indeed interesting that so many characteristic thirties preoccupations— education, employment, health, social welfare, communications, a rational transport system — were in fact among the principal political themes of post-1945 Britain; and surely the kind of thinking that had been done in the thirties, whether by composers, poets, economists, pamphleteers, psychologists, statisticians or politicians, proved to be extremely influential in the post-war period. It may be paradoxical to suggest, but it might possibly prove to be true, that the thirties' finest *political* hour was not achieved until the forties and fifties, which is another reason for seeing the period as part of a continuum, not as a self-contained, watertight episode. It is also a view that establishes a connection between the reformist socialism of post-1945 and the traditional liberal values which formed so important a part of the eccentric political mix characteristic of the thirties.

I have already quoted from Britten's diaries—his remark about *Our Hunting Fathers* being his 'real' Op. 1. (His Op. 1 was in fact his already published *Sinfonietta*.) How lucky for us that as a boy, youth and up-and-coming composer he was such a methodical diarist. He kept mainly pocket diaries, making daily entries, sometimes very short, sometimes quite long, from the year 1928, when he was aged fourteen, until 1938, when the entry for 16 June proved to be the last. The existence of these diaries, which in my view are without doubt one of the major manuscript sources for students of the period — not just for students of the composer —

enables us to come as close as is humanly possible to knowing what it was like to be an artist in the thirties, not only as a developing artist however, but also as a young man in a wide variety of contexts. At the centre there was the family; and then radiating outwards, multiple series of personal relationships, of collaborations with individuals and organizations, of involvement in the great contentious issues of the day. There is also, not least, a powerful sense of aspiration, of ambition, and an exceptionally practical awareness of the necessity to work, to keep one's financial end up and not sink down among the overdrafts. The work-ethic must certainly rate very high among the young Britten's inborn characteristics: it was something he retained to the very end of his life. [3]

In following the progress of 1936 through Britten's diary for that year we find ourselves on the *inside* of the thirties rather than the outside. We have access to the topical thoughts — written down it would seem never later than the next day, and without much sifting or screening (Britten was remarkably open and frank with himself about himself, and about his friends)—of an artist wholly committed to a career that at very many critical points touched on major aspects of the creative life of the thirties. As we read the diary entries, with all their immediacy—this, we feel, *was* how it was— the distorting perspective provided by the 'completed view' of history is absent. The diaries give us history, or at least one man's history, in the making. The availability of the diaries, and of the associated musical works, the creation (and conception) of which the diaries record, gives us a means of access to the very heart of the period denied most scholars and biographers. Above all, the diaries, quite apart from the invaluable chronological documentation they provide of the composition of Britten's works during this period—not to speak of the light they throw on his youthful working methods—show us that ambiguous relationship between the private and public life which Professor Hynes has, again I think rightly, singled out as a feature of the thirties, and which is emphatically relevant to any consideration of Britten, both as an artist and as a man.

It is a curious fact — though perhaps it is really not curious at all but simply further confirmation of the integrity of his artistic personality — that in the shaping of so much of his work, long after the thirties, and when indeed the music from that period was wholly unfamiliar to audiences, and perhaps even relegated to the back of the composer's own mind, an old tension persisted: how to keep in balance, in proportion, a sense of responsibility to society, to a community, with the need to fulfil himself as an artist, that is, to *live*, not construct, his experience. The sense of social responsibility was always a powerful motivation for Britten and should, I suggest, be properly regarded as part of his legacy from the thirties, but like Aschenbach, in Britten's last opera *Death in Venice*, the artist, the creator, has to say: 'So be it!';[4] and surrender himself to ingesting the personal, private experience without which his art is sterile. The friction generated by the private/public dichotomy is a fruitful one, particularly in Britten's case. We encounter it repeatedly throughout his work.

The private/public theme had been raised as early as 1927, in Auden's preface to *Oxford Poetry* of that year, where he wrote: 'All genuine poetry is in a sense the formation of private spheres out of a public chaos. . . .'[5] This was, as Professor Hynes points out, 'the first assertion of a theme that recurs throughout the thirties, and embodies one of the central literary problems of the period — the relation between public and private experience in literature at a time of public disorder, the "Private faces / In public places" theme that Auden put in his epigraph to *The Orators*'.[6] One could argue of course that there was nothing particularly new in this private/public dichotomy, that in some form or other it has almost always played a role in art—indeed, that the friction between, the intersecting of, private and public world is an inseparable part of the human condition, at least in all contexts where man emerges in any degree as a social animal. But perhaps there was a sense in which the private/public juxtaposition was given altogether fresh impetus and emphasis in the thirties, and particularly by the generation of thirties artists, who saw it as part of their social obligation *as* artists to concern themselves with public affairs, with the political events of the day.[7] It was this conscious acceptance of a political/social obligation by so many of them that seems to me to spell out the old private/public conflict in a new way.

Although it is true that Auden was later to change his mind and to adopt the view—which, I think, Britten never came to share— that art was powerless to change the world, to modify human behaviour, he did not always think in quite that way. Indeed, it is clear from his introduction to the anthology he edited in 1935 with John Garrett, *The Poet's Tongue*,[8] that while he always maintained a distance from the concept of art as propaganda, he was firm in his belief, at that time at least, in the educative function of art, or even perhaps in the moral power of art. 'There must', wrote Auden, 'always be two kinds of art, escape-art, for man needs escape as he needs food and deep sleep, and parable-art, that art which shall teach man to unlearn hatred and learn love. . . .'[9] Of course, as Professor Hynes rightly comments, that is in itself some sort of political statement; if not exactly a political programme, it is still a programme in which the artist has a practical role to play.[10] Moreover it is envisaged that the artist can properly hope through his 'parables' — a concept of special relevance to any consideration of Britten's art, who so often used parable as one of his prime working methods; and I am thinking here of not just his three Church Parables (1964–68) but of his *oeuvre* as a whole — to effect the kind of changes in human relationships that will bring about a more decent, more just, better-ordered society. In short, it was a reformist policy, very much in the established English liberal tradition, and tied in significantly with the notion of art as an agent of change through the education of the heart. Professor Hynes is surely right to point to 'change of heart' as another of the key phrases of the thirties:[11] as Auden put it, 'New styles of architecture, a change of heart'.[12]

That 'change of heart', for many of the most talented spirits of the thirties, meant striving for a change of political heart; and the most vocal and articulate political point of view that was available was represented by the newly fledged Communist Party, that Professor Hynes does well to remind us was itself of very recent origin as far as the UK was concerned:

The Communist Party of Great Britain had been in existence for less than ten years when the decade began—like disillusionment, it was a post-war phenomenon. The *Daily Worker* began publication in 1930, and the *Left Review*, which was the nearest thing to an official organ that the intellectuals of the Left had, did not appear until 1934. The whole question of what a British Communist would be — how he would behave, what he would think about art and literature, and what kind he would himself produce if he were an artist—all these questions were unanswered, even unasked, in 1930. The thirties was not a time of political orthodoxy, but a time when orthodoxy was being worked out. . . .[13]

That is a timely caution, well worth spelling out here because it reminds us of two important considerations: first, that there was distinctly an air of newness about the Communist Party—it was not retailing the tired old political package of the day—and second, the very fluidity of thinking in the area of the arts, the flexibility, the comparative absence of dogma, meant that basically independent spirits, independent-minded creators like Britten and Auden, were able to work within the general context of left-wing politics on projects, or for causes, with which they were undeniably in sympathy but without necessarily committing themselves to a party line — because for the arts at least, there was no party line, or at best only an exiguous one. The field, as it were, was an open one. Given the presence of sentiments and sympathies that were generally inclined towards the Left, one worked where one chose and how one chose, choices no doubt governed by what one thought one's best capacities or most effective contribution might be. Thus the Communist Party was not, or at least not for the many artists who formed a constellation about it, a coherent body of belief. Rather it provided a rallying point, a centre of protest radiating outwards and representing at its periphery many individual voices, perhaps in general sympathy, but certainly not in unison.[14] And after all, with a dispirited National Government lacking credibility and an incoherent, fractured Labour Party, what other rallying point was there for protesting radicals — or, for that matter, moderates—of the day? It is not surprising in these circumstances, and bearing in mind the persecution of the radical Left in Europe at the time, which understandably engaged the attention and aroused the indignation of so many artists, that the Communist Party seemed to offer both a flag and an umbrella: a shelter under which many disparate and even divided talents might temporarily gather together.[15]

One worked where one chose. Where and how Britten chose to work—the kind of musical choices he made—tell us a lot about him and about the period. We also begin to learn I think how, in fact, a period is 'made'—by artists and others creating the characteristic forms and shapes by which, retrospectively, we can recognize the distinctive nature of a particular period. The thirties was a period rich in innovatory forms, especially those associated with theatre, film and radio. In these areas as a *maker* of the thirties, Britten, like Auden, emerges by any reckoning as a major figure. It is disconcerting that even a study as admirable as Professor Hynes's, which sets out to give a comprehensive account of the Auden generation, should have no entry for Britten in its index and make only one brief mention of him in the text (in connection with the film *Night Mail*). Music, as we shall see, was a peculiarly vital aspect of the media associated with the thirties; and it was often Britten's that was the 'voice' through which this significant dimension of thirties art made itself audible. But what the thirties did give Britten, which he might never have gained in another period, a different decade, was a quite remarkable training which in many specific ways prepared the great flowering of his art in the mid-1940s. In that sense, at least, one of the makers of the thirties had a debt to pay to the decade of which he was part.

One worked where one chose. One was also chosen. How Britten stood at the very beginning of 1936 in relation to his career is set out in the first entry of his new diary. It was his invariable custom to survey himself and his affairs at the start of a new year and his introduction to 1936 reads like this:

1936 finds me infinitely better off in all ways than did the beginning of 1935; it finds me earning my living — with occasionally something to spare—at the G.P.O. film Unit under John Grierson & [Alberto] Cavalcanti, writing music & supervising sounds for films (this one G.P.O. Night Mail) at the rate of £5 per week, but owing to the fact I can claim no performing rights (it being Crown property) with the possibility of it being increased to £10 per week or £2 per day; writing very little, but with the possibility & ideas for writing a lot of original music, as I am going under an agreement with Boosey & Hawkes for a £3 a week guarantee of royalties; having a lot of success but not a staggering amount of performances, the reputation (even for bad) growing steadily; having a bad inferiority complex in company of brains like Basil Wright, Wystan Auden & William Coldstream; being fortunate in friends like Mr & Mrs Frank Bridge, Henry Boys, Basil Reeve (& young Piers Dunkeley—tell it not in Gath) and afar off Francis Barton,[16] being comfortably settled in a pleasant, tho' cold flat in West Hampstead[17] with Beth [Britten],[18] with whom I get on very well; doing much housework but with prospect of having a woman in more than twice a week in evenings & once in mornings.

'So for 1936' is the final phrase of the first entry, a typical mixture of domesticity, financial reckoning, creative activities and plans, and self-assessment. That 'bad inferiority complex' will prove to be a recurrent theme. We also notice that Wystan Auden is already installed on the first page. He is to make increasingly frequent appearances as the year progresses.

While, as the preamble to his 1936 diary makes clear, Britten was to be heavily engaged in his work for the GPO Film Unit — the work which earned him his living and which formed part of his social environment, and also represented the discharge of his responsibilities as artisan–artist—there was, as well, however, all that 'original' music to be written. By 'original' Britten meant, I think, to distinguish music other than that written on demand for film, radio or theatre; and on 2 January, indeed, after a first day of the year that was largely spent hanging about for Basil Wright to appear for a discussion of the *Night Mail* film project (the meeting seems to have taken place next day), we encounter the first mention of what in every sense of the word was to turn out to be an 'original' piece of work, what might be argued to be one of the most original of all his compositions—*Our Hunting Fathers*. At this stage, of course, the project has no title, and is slipped like this into the texture of the entry:

> Auden comes back here [to the West Hampstead flat] for a meal at 7.30. We talk amongst many things of a new Song Cycle (probably on Animals) that I may write. Very nice and interesting & pleasant evening.

The day had opened very differently, and I quote the whole passage because it shows very clearly the mix of activities that was the staple diet of Britten's working day at this time, a mix of professional undertakings — the GPO Film Unit on the one hand, kicking off with a new 'original' project on the other — with a dash of family life injected for good measure:

> Go to Soho Square in morning to work with Auden & Wright on G.P.O.—the first 'correction' of our Tuesday's work. Meet Robert [Britten][19] (on his way back to Prestatyn with Marjorie & John)[20] & Beth for lunch at Lyons' new Marble Arch Corner House (esp. for R's benefit). To Blackheath in aft. with Wright & Auden for 2nd 'correction' (now completely altered) of G.P.O. work — by [Harry] Watt (director of film).

So much for the morning and afternoon, both spent on *Night Mail*, with a domestic interlude for lunch and the first discussion of *Our Hunting Fathers* in the evening. As we shall see, by Britten's standards this was a pretty average and not especially hard-pressed day. The creative counterpoint is altogether fascinating and typical, not only because of the factual detail — we can follow the progress of a project, of a composition, day by day and sometimes almost hour by hour — but because we come to see very clearly how the 'public' works, i.e. the music written for the GPO Film Unit, the BBC, the Group Theatre, the Left Revue, etc., music committed to a particular enterprise, and the 'private' works — what Britten referred to in his verbal overture to 1936 as 'original' music — were written as it were in tandem. To put it another way, if we think of the two main areas of Britten's creative activity as hoops, then both were kept bowling along simultaneously. Most illuminating of all are the frequent occasions on which the two hoops overlap and intersect. There is an intriguing relationship to be explored between the 'original' projects and the commissioned works, what one might call social utility pieces, with techniques developed under high pressure in the latter field undoubtedly consolidating and augmenting the resources on which Britten could call when exercising his 'private' imagination.

As we proceed we shall become increasingly aware of witnessing a young composer applying his craft most vigorously and with the utmost versatility to every challenge that presented itself and seemed to offer interesting possibilities. Thus the picture we have of Britten in the thirties is not only one of achievement, of an image-maker of and for the period, but also of a highly gifted young composer voraciously learning a multiplicity of crafts, and assembling a huge stock of techniques which were not only of immediate use but were to prove of lasting value. In fact there are two highly significant interrelationships involved here. The interpenetration of the private and public spheres is one; the other, no less important, is the relationship that with hindsight we can now discern between the fields in which Britten chose to work at this time and his later development as a composer. There are many examples of this last relationship between his activities in the thirties and future paths that were still unknown to him: to take only one obvious instance, the more we study what he was contributing to the thirties, and above all the immense amount of creative energy and skill he poured into dramatic forms of various kinds — incidental music for the theatre, radio features, film scores — the less surprising it becomes that he was to emerge in the mid-1940s as the leading musical dramatist of his generation. It was the thirties that provided him with just the training that quite peculiarly fitted him for the bold dramatic ventures of his later life. Seen in this context, the assurance, expertise and confidence, the sheer dramatic knack and flair, that marked *Peter Grimes* must strike one not as qualities conjured out of the air but as manifestations of techniques that had been prepared over a long period in the often gruelling environment of a film studio, cutting-room or theatre pit.

It was on 2 January that Auden and Britten had first dicussed a cycle of songs 'on Animals'; and now in March, the texts were beginning to arrive from Auden. It is not surprising, I think, that Britten shows these to Frank Bridge, his old teacher and mentor, with whom the bonds were still strong. I can well imagine that Britten wanted the older man's assurance that he too shared some of his pupil's enthusiasm for his poet collaborator, who was beginning to loom ever larger in Britten's musical life. The assurance, fortunately, was forthcoming:

> 23 MARCH:
> As it is fearfully wet [at Friston][21] all the morning — spend it talking to F.B. Very interesting & deep conversation — I show him Auden's stuff for me and he is impressed. Also find he is very sympathetic towards my socialistic inclinations, in fact we are in complete agreement over all — except Mahler! — though he admits he [Mahler] is a great thinker.

Auden must have been busy on his own account, what with his own private and public writing—the distinction one makes for Britten can, I think, be made for Auden too—with assembling the texts for *Our Hunting Fathers*, and also thinking, no doubt, about what shape the new play he was to write with Christopher Isherwood, *The Ascent of F6*, might take. In any event, the decision to involve Britten in the making of *F6* was clearly taken at an early stage; and within a few days of his approaching Bridge about 'Auden's stuff' for the new song-cycle, he had a letter from the poet 'asking me to do music for his and Isherwood's new play'. At first Britten had some doubts about the possibility of fitting the work into his schedule. But as we know the music for *F6* did get written, and the play was first performed on 26 February 1937. It was not, however, until October 1936 that Britten received the text of the new play, and during the spring and the entire summer, from April to August, he was wholly preoccupied with his current collaboration with Auden, with the composition and completion of the 'big songs', as he referred to them in his diary — the orchestral song-cycle on animals, *Our Hunting Fathers*, that had been on the stocks since January.

The first performance of this ambitious work had already been planned: it was to take place at the Norwich Festival on 25 September, with the composer himself conducting. There were obviously good reasons for choosing Norwich to launch a work that must have struck a fair number among the audience as a musical missile: there were Frank Bridge's links with the Festival, as conductor and composer, and so his star pupil was following in his footsteps; and of course Britten was himself an East Anglian. However, it seems possible that a certain perturbation was evident at Norwich when the proposal was raised initially, no doubt due to the subject of the song-cycle, for Britten records what must have been a somewhat uncomfortable lunch in February, on the 18th:

> . . . at Victoria with Mr. Graham Goodes (the very objectionable, self-important, bumptious and altogether despicable secretary of the Norwich Festival). I find it most difficult to make him come round to letting me do a vocal suite (Sophie Wyss) for the Sept. festival. In fact, I'm convinced it was only to give himself airs that he ever queried it.

So, *Our Hunting Fathers* was on.

The three central poems Auden chose for *Our Hunting Fathers* were Thomas Ravenscroft's 'Dance of Death' ('Hawking for the Partridge') and two texts by anonymous poets, 'Rats Away!' and 'Messalina'. Auden modernized 'Rats Away!' and added his own Epilogue, from which the song-cycle derives its title, a poem which had first been published in 1934, and early in 1936 he wrote a Prologue specifically for the song-cycle.[22] Britten, as we have learned from his diary, thought of the work as a cycle of songs 'on Animals'; and undoubtedly the complex relationship of man to the animals, an awareness that the world was shared by both animals and men, that men had something to learn from animals—these were preoccupations of Auden's which indeed were to emerge again in a later musical collaboration with Britten, the operetta *Paul Bunyan*,[23] composed in America (1940–41), where animals are among the principal characters: Fido, a dog, and Moppet and Poppet, two cats (a high soprano and two mezzos). About these unusual members of *Bunyan's* cast there is much that might be said: for example, in the very moving Litany that brings the operetta to a close, it is the dog and the two cats who catalogue a series of Audenesque social ills:

> From a Pressure Group that says I am the Constitution,
> From those who say Patriotism and mean Persecution,
> From a Tolerance that is really inertia and delusion . . .

to which the chorus responds, 'Save animals and men',[24] showing a nice touch of politeness in the order of priorities and perhaps also indicating the poet's preference. But it is on the animals in *Our Hunting Fathers* that I must concentrate. The three middle songs of the cycle, 'Rats Away!', 'Messalina' and 'Dance of Death', are quite clearly associated with animals and men in contrasted contexts. The Prologue and Epilogue, Auden's own texts, which frame the cycle, place the central songs in a philosophical perspective (though I use the word 'philosophical' with no particular confidence, so baffling, on the whole, do I find Auden's words). But while it is certainly the case that the frame was intended to prevent the audience from interpreting the central songs too literally, too pictorially, the actual songs themselves also far transcend the topics and situations they seem outwardly to depict. Indeed, a wealth of symbolism is involved, a multiplicity of levels of comprehension; and at least one of those levels was bound up with the politics of the day, the politics of 1936.

As we shall see, Britten's diaries for the period when he was actually putting *Our Hunting Fathers* together are unusually full of political comments and observations, some samples of which I shall be quoting. The particular tensions and anxieties of the summer of 1936 formed part of the imagination out of which *Our Hunting Fathers* was created, and although I speak of imagination in the singular, it is Auden's and Britten's fused imaginations that I have in mind. But yet more specific and revealing, I suggest, is the choice of texts, which in very subtle ways are made to develop a dimension to their imagery which was certainly not part of the original texts; and the agent of re-interpretation, the provider of the new dimension, was often the music. This is particularly true of the first song, 'Rats Away!', and true in a particularly interesting way; and since it was with 'Rats Away!' that Britten started work — not with the framing Prologue and Epilogue (and perhaps the opaqueness of Auden's texts was at least part of the reason why Britten postponed tackling the beginning and end of the cycle) — I intend to take 'Rats Away!' as my first example.

It was one of those celebrated pre-compositional walks— celebrated, because they became a permanent feature of Britten's working method — on Hampstead Heath on 12 May 1936, that got 'Rats Away!' going:

> Go for a tremendous walk over Hampstead Heath practically all the morning — after an energetic practice — trying to finish 'Rats' in my mind. But it won't work — it is a pig. I get back for lunch & settle down to think in the afternoon — but infinite telephone calls distract me entirely & I eventually go off to tennis at 5.30.

For the next three days, work on the song went well and speedily. But on 19 May, Britten turned to the second of the three central songs, 'Messalina': 'Rats Away!' was sticking. A good moment, perhaps, while Britten himself makes no progress, for us to look at 'Rats Away!' But, first, why 'Rats'? Why *vermin*?

I think this is where, in an oblique way maybe, although I think it is absolutely clear how we are meant to take the image, Auden and Britten presented a sharp-toothed view of their world in 1936, and more especially of the political world which surrounded them: society and civilization assailed by rats, and particularly by Fascist rats, in Spain, Germany, and, in the month that Britten started 'Rats Away!', Italy:

4/5 MAY 1936:
The Italian-Abyssinian war is nearing its close. Addis-Ababa is in a

state of confusion, the Emperor (fine man) has fled & most of his generals & what with Italians and native looters it is in a bad way. Mussolini's war of civilisation is at an end. What country will be in need of treatment now?

One does not, I think, need actually to spell out the symbolism in detail, because then the concept begins to sound crude. But given the situation at home and abroad in 1936, and the prevailing conviction among so many intellectuals that Europe and European culture were done for, a prayer to rid the world of a plague of rats must have seemed strikingly appropriate. English satire has often tended to be less fierce, less overtly politicized, than its European counterpart, but Britten's and Auden's 'Rats Away!' is very sharp indeed and imagined in sound that, as we shall see, has a no less sharp edge to it. Thus can music embody an attitude, a point of view, which need not necessarily be part of the meaning of the original text. It seems probable that among the ideas that Britten had in his head on his walk on 12 May was the musical image of the rats themselves: the brilliant opening pages of the song are made up of tiny ladders of ascending scale motives, spread throughout the whole orchestra, which gradually invade the total texture, a striking evocation of rats let loose, and piercingly shrill in timbre.

It is out of the basic idea of the ascending scale motive that the song is built; and in case we have not ourselves made the association between the motive and the animal, the first entry of the voice makes it clear. We are presented with a vocal version of the opening orchestral gestures, in which the soloist makes the tiny ladders continuous and melismatically projects the key word, 'Rats!':

Ex. 1

I think we may be confident that nothing quite like this music had been heard before in the UK of 1936. The orchestral writing alone was exceptional; and remember that this was in fact Britten's first work in which a large orchestra was involved. The instrumentation is a point to which I shall be returning, but for the moment let me offer one word that does something, I believe, to describe its exceptional character: virtuosity. We are now accustomed to virtuoso instrumental writing, but in 1936, amid the dense pastoral and, above all, vague orchestral textures so much favoured by some senior English composers of the day, it was possible for an *admiring* pupil to write of Ralph Vaughan Williams: 'He was an instinctive poet in music and at that time had a horror of professional skill and technical ability.'[25] It was, alas, a view that generated an influential and enduring suspiciousness of virtuosity in English musical life. Small wonder that the youthful Britten's dazzling clarity and precision sounded arresting to those who liked it, and extremely uncomfortable, impertinent and provoking to those who did not. Moreover, on top of that, there was his no less innovatory approach to the voice. There had not been vocal writing of this particular order for a very long time in English music. As that extraordinary vocal flourish—almost a cadenza—on 'Rats!' shows, Britten restores to the voice an energy and virtuosity of technique that had come to be thought of as the province of the instrumentalist rather than the singer. But in *Our Hunting Fathers*, as 'Rats Away!' makes clear from the start, the voice is required to be as agile as any instrument; indeed, the voice is treated by Britten as if it were another instrument among his instrumental resources, and he makes demands of it accordingly. (After the first performance *The Times* reacted to all this virtuosity as if it were an attack of childhood measles: '. . . if it is a stage to be got through, we wish [the composer] safely and quickly through it.')

But let me return to the song and its musical organization. The idea of 'Rats!' having been established orchestrally and vocally, the soloist then embarks on the mock prayer that enjoins the saints to exorcise the rats. The scale motive, those ascending ladders of notes, associated firmly in our minds with the rats themselves, has no role to play in the texture of this part of the song:

Ex. 2

One might imagine that the prayer is efficacious, and indeed there is nothing in Auden's version of the text to tell us whether the exorcism works or not. It is precisely at this point that the music, as it were, steps in and makes a point that lends a fresh dimension to the text. As the prayer comes to an end, not only does the woodwind figuration begin to scamper and to re-form itself into scalic patterns, though still relatively unobtrusively, but a baleful tuba solo is added to the texture, the most subversive and menacing sound of all. I write I confess with hindsight, but then so may all of us who have heard *Death in Venice*, where it is the sonority of the tuba that acts, as it were, as the bearer of the plague, the symbolic and actual plague that kills Aschenbach. How extraordinary that already in 1936 it was the tuba that was associated in Britten's inner imagination with the idea of pestilence:

Ex. 3

Knowing that, which shows if nothing else the consistency of Britten's instrumental symbolism, it is hardly surprising that at the moment of recapitulation, which is also the last statement of the prayer, the rats reappear, interrupting, invading and infiltrating the prayer itself, so that it becomes madly infested with the

ascending scale motive, which finally has restored to it the importance and continuity it had at the beginning of the song:

Ex. 4

There is an ironic and subdued 'Amen' from the singer but the
orchestra's ensuing brilliant and unbroken scale leaves us in no
doubt that it is the rats who have triumphed and not the prayer.[27]
This particular passage is not only a highly ingenious recapitulation
performing the necessary musical function of restatement, albeit in
a mocking form, but it also introduces, through purely musical
means, a symbolic and dramatic meaning which the text alone
certainly does not offer. The image of humankind swamped by
vermin and in peril of defeat—the old nostrums having lost their
power—remains a very potent one. It must have seemed especially
relevant to the youthful Auden and Britten in the summer of 1936.

Quite apart from the implied political symbolism of *Our Hunting
Fathers*, which I am sure was already surfacing in 'Rats Away!',
there was also undoubtedly an intent to shock at a more direct and
indeed local level. *Our Hunting Fathers* also took as its target those
members of English society for whom 'the hunt' represented a way
of life, an inviolable tradition, especially of course in rural
England. It can scarcely have escaped Auden's and Britten's notice
that the Norwich Festival took place in one of the hearts of rural
England and was likely to be attended and supported by the local

gentry whose hunting habits and customs were to come under scrutiny in their song-cycle 'on Animals'.[28] Small wonder that the Secretary of the Festival, about whom Britten was so scornful, showed some nervousness when the project was outlined to him. One wonders what Mr Goodes made of 'Rats Away!' We know what Mrs Britten made of it, because there is an entry in the composer's diary which records her reaction:

> After dinner I play it [the day's work] over a lot & describe it [*Our Hunting Fathers*] in detail to Mum. She disapproves very thoroughly of 'Rats'—but that is almost an incentive—no actual insult to her tho'.

That Britten found his mother's disapproval something of 'an incentive' tells us a good deal about the kind of attitudes and opinions it was at least part of the intention of the co-authors of *Our Hunting Fathers* to shake at Norwich later in the year.

Lest anyone should mistake virtuosity for mere facility, it is worth pointing out, I think, that 'Rats Away!' cost Britten a great deal in toil and sweat to get it right. As we have seen, he declared himself stuck on 19 May and took up 'Messalina', the lament for a dead monkey. 'Rats Away!' was resumed again on 3 June, and a first sketch of the song finished that day, but — the diary concludes — 'much to be altered still'. For the next few days, there seemed to be little but slogging away with only partial success at both 'Messalina' and 'Rats Away!'

Despite—or perhaps because of—the difficulties with 'Rats Away!' and 'Messalina', Britten began thinking about 'Hawking' (finally to be entitled 'Dance of Death'), the setting of Ravenscroft's poem 'Hawking for the Partridge', on the 8th and made a start on the song on the 9th. But, like the preceding songs, 'Hawking' sticks, until 11 June when there is clearly some kind of breakthrough:

> Work at Hawking morning & afternoon & on a walk after tea. Lovely day, tho' cold evening. Work goes much better, indeed I feel quite cheerful—almost excited—about it later in the day.

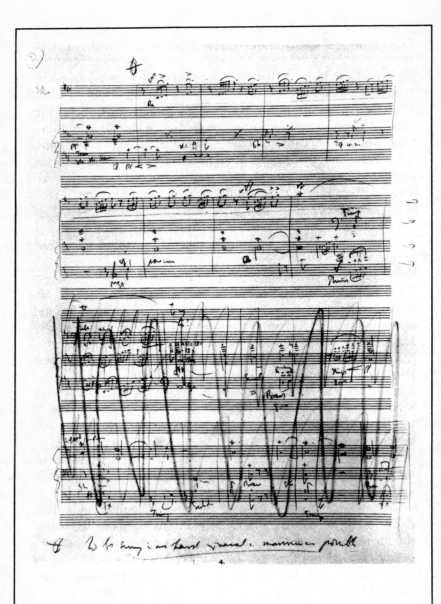

2 A page from Britten's pencil sketches for 'Rats Away!' from *Our Hunting Fathers* © The Britten Estate

In fact Britten's optimism proves to be false. The very next day 'Hawking' goes wrong again:

> Work goes very badly. I am stuck at the middle of Hawking — not actually stuck because I write a tremendous amount all of which is no bon.

I am not going to pursue every stop and go that marked the composing of *Our Hunting Fathers*. But I have deliberately gone into a little of the detail of the compositional chronology and of the sheer compositional labour involved in getting things right in order to demonstrate something that is so often ignored, perhaps especially in the case of a composer like Britten, whose music sounds so unlaboured. And yet his diaries prove that that very quality of spontaneity was an aspect of a virtuoso technique that had to be worked at as hard as at any other and often took a significant time to achieve.

However, with our composer stuck again, not only in 'Rats Away!', but also in 'Hawking', perhaps it is the appropriate moment for us to look at 'Messalina', the slow centre of the triptych, which Britten had managed to complete to his satisfaction. It is perhaps the only part of the song-cycle which might be said to explore the kind of relationship between men and animals—in this case between Messalina and her dying pet monkey—on which most people would doubtless have expected a song-cycle 'on Animals' to have spent a fair amount of its time. 'Messalina', especially after 'Rats Away!', must have struck a more sympathetic note in the audience at the première; but even so, the hugeness of Messalina's grief at the loss of her monkey, so overwhelming, so passionate a torrent of grieving—was there not something faintly unseemly about this disproportion? This storm of sorrow—over a *monkey*? Once again, the music, by audaciously inverting the scale of the feeling and discharging it with such irresistible conviction—by converting the sentiment of the poem into a torrential paroxysm of grief—adds a wholly new dimension to the text: the shock of it should shake one into a new perception of what men and animals might mean to each other. And, again, an extravagant cadenza on the word — no, the sound — 'Fie', represents the innovatory vocal style that is characteristic of *Our Hunting Fathers*:

Ex. 5

One final point: so intense is the release of grief in the vocal cadenza, that it has to be wound down through a sequence of cadenzas for solo wind—flute to oboe—to clarinet—to alto saxophone, with each cadenza unerringly imagined for the character of the instrument as it surfaces with its own version of Messalina's lamenting. For its time, a daring approach to scoring for an orchestra of soloists, at least part of which Britten had learnt from Mahler. (Incidentally, 'Messalina' exists in a setting by Thomas Weelkes, an ayre for three voices, published in 1608. It is quite likely that Britten would have known of this distinguished precedent: for a time he was a keen madrigalist in the thirties.)

But whatever we may think of Messalina and her monkey, the second song of *Our Hunting Fathers* undoubtedly celebrates a world of private sorrow. With the onset of the· third song, 'Hawking' — 'Dance of Death' — we move back, I suggest, into the public world, and specifically into the world of 1936. This time, I think, Auden's and Britten's commentary on topical events, though still achieved through symbolic means, is a good deal more

explicit than it was in 'Rats Away!' It is true of course that 'Hawking'
presents the conventional theme of animals hunted by man:
animals as prey, thus adding a third to the themes of the first two
songs, animals as pests and pets. But while 'Dance of Death' is
indeed a song of 'the killing of animals for pleasure',[29] as Peter Pears
has described it, it is also more than that, a song of savagery and
persecution. In the context of 1936 I have no doubt at all that it was
the persecution of the Jews by the Nazis in Germany that Auden
and Britten had in mind when devising this 'Dance of Death'. This
is not, I hope to show, all speculation.

   The song opens with one of the most extraordinary passages
Britten was ever to write for the solo voice. Again, the virtuoso,
instrumental treatment of the voice was unprecedented. Britten
explores to their limits the resources of vocal timbre, attack,
colour and dynamics, with an exact technical perception of what
the voice is capable of producing, as it were, under pressure.
Indeed, this opening passage—which Britten *scores* for the voice,
as if it were not one voice but a multiple instrumental resource—
remains one of the boldest in all his music. The text itself is no less
original in its way: a kind of sound-track of the calls and whistles
associated with hawking, a litany of the hawks' (or is it the retrieving
hounds'?)[30] names, interrupted by huntsmen's whoops and the
strange whistle—'Whurret'—which Britten scores as an ascending glissando on a rolled 'r' across the span of a minor ninth. It is
with a roll call, *sotto voce*, that the 'Dance of Death' opens: 'Duty,
Quando, Travel, Jew' and then 'Beauty, Timble, Trover, Damsel,
Duty, Quando, Travel, Jew':

Ex. 6

After that startling opening, the hunt — the hawking — begins; and for his 'Dance of Death' Britten uses precisely the same kind of compositional techniques that were a feature of 'Rats Away!', especially with regard to the vocal writing, above all in the rolled 'r' whistles that invade and decorate the vocal line—a clear parallel with the scale motive that festoons the voice part in the recapitulation of 'Rats Away!'—and in what one might think of as a development section, in which those haunting names are treated melismatically, emerging as rising and falling arches of sound. I use the word 'development' advisedly; because one of the interesting aspects of that arresting opening passage for solo voice is that it exposes virtually all the principal ideas out of which a very long movement is built. A virtuoso, acrobatic passage maybe, but as we find in the music of all good composers, fireworks, however brilliant, always have a precise formal function. In the development of that strange roll call, Britten recreates the veritable sound–world of hawking. This was a section of the song, I think, which more than once had frustrated his efforts to complete it satisfactorily.[31]

If we are to return to the symbolic dimension of *Our Hunting Fathers* and its relevance to public affairs in the thirties, as poet and composer saw them, it is once more to the music that we must look if we are to find the transcending commentary. We find it, I suggest, in the 'Dance of Death' itself, for orchestra alone. This is a self-contained development section for which the musical precedent is very clearly the great developmental march for orchestra alone which is the centre-piece of 'Der Abschied' in Mahler's *Das Lied von der Erde*, a work well-known to Britten at this time: he was in fact one of the earliest of Mahler's champions in England. As in the comparable passage in Mahler's finale, the voice is silent in Britten's 'Dance of Death' and, thus freed from any obligations to the text, the composer can, as it were, speak directly through his notes. And I am certain that in this remarkable section Britten puts all thought of local parody and satire behind him and composes out of the full experience of the dance of death that was already under way on the continent of Europe and in Africa. It was only a few days after finishing 'Hawking' that Britten was writing this in his diary, on Friday, 26 June:

> I like Fridays because apart from the daily paper there is the Radio Times (occasionally World Radio too) & New Statesman. All good to read, tho' no news is good to read now. The government have definitely decided to stop sanctions — on the principle that Abyssinia is lost & nothing will bring her back again. Forgetting entirely the punitive value of them. Alas for collective security. If Mussolini can get away with it, what for Hitler? O God, this National Government!

The 'Dance of Death' represents the peak of orchestral virtuosity that *Our Hunting Fathers* attains — we have to remind ourselves that we are listening to music by a composer not yet twenty-three — and it comprises a ferocious transformation of the music hitherto associated with the hunt. Britten has been careful throughout to maintain a link with the galloping rhythm of traditional hunting music, and does so still in this orchestral passage which is not only the climax of the hunt but also, in musical terms, a strict development—this time, however, it is the orchestra which is the soloist—of materials exposed by the voice at the outset of the song. This great orchestral eruption brings us to the very brink of chaos and disintegration; and in it, Britten moves furthest from tonality and into dissonant textures that embody the strains and tensions of the dance to death and destruction.[32]

Some of the most vivid of the political entries in Britten's diaries were made while he was scoring *Our Hunting Fathers*, the final stage in the composition of the work for which he announced himself to be ready on 27 June. The scoring of 'Hawking', of the

'Dance of Death', was done in July, between the 11th (the day on which he finished scoring 'Rats Away!') and the 21st. It was a period when he was reading Karl Marx—'After dinner read a lot more Marx. Hard going though edifying'—and when the news from Spain took precedence in the diary. On the day he completed the scoring of the whole work—23 July—he wrote:

> Rather a beastly day—spoilt by Spanish news. There has been a lot more fighting & the Government doesn't seem entirely on top— there seems to be a lot of dirty work going on—rich people outside helping those bloody fascists. There has been a lot of fighting round Barcelona—and hundreds are dead.
>   I actually finish the score of H.F. working till 11.30 at night— owing to these disturbances I don't work well & I'm very doubtful about the end.

And again, on the 24th, this entry:

> News from Spain still bad, tho' government seems to be gaining ground a bit—it varies with what paper one reads. One thing is certain is that Fascists are executing hundreds (literally) of Popular Front or Communist members—including many boys of 14–16. Marvellous to have opinions of that strength at that age. I can't help feeling that not until that 'political consciousness' is more general that the world will get out of this mess.

Not even the horror of the Spanish Civil War could entirely diminish Britten's own sense of achievement and exultation at having reached the end of the 'big songs', and he adds, in words which remind us of his youthfulness, and of that necessary detachment an artist must have if he is to create positively and take joy in his creativity, even in negative circumstances:

> Apart from that I am exhilarated at having finished Hunting Fathers. Spend day—numbering pages, doing titles, index, cueing, general expression & tempo marks etc.—which is good fun, especially as I am at the moment thrilled with the work.

Those political comments can represent only the tip of the iceberg; and it is impossible to quantify what influence topical events had on the composition of *Our Hunting Fathers*, on the actual composing process. However, those quotations speak for Britten's awareness of his own times, not only *in* which, but *for* which, he was creating, and I am convinced that some part of that awareness, of a political conscience as well as consciousness, was built into the 'Dance of Death' so powerfully imagined for orchestra in July 1936.

But, amid so much speculation, how much evidence is there to justify *Our Hunting Fathers* being considered in some substantial sense as a politically engaged work? There is the general symbolism of the hunt and there is 'Jew' included in the litany of names— although the hawks and hounds are, after all, the hunters, not the hunted. 'Jew', as I have pointed out, is among the first names we hear. Much later in the song, as one of the names that Britten treats melismatically in his middle section, a new name appears: 'German'. Both names, by the way, appear in the original Ravenscroft text: they were not introduced by Auden. But it seems to me that the matter is clinched if we pay attention to the work itself; for there we find a clue which enables us, I believe, to interpret the 'Dance of Death' as I have suggested and with some confidence in the correctness of the approach. Because, although the dance is purely orchestral, it actually discharges into a vocal coda, a tailpiece, in which the 'whurret' whistle frames just two words, two names. One has to listen intently, and of course to be quick on the uptake, to catch the message, which so to speak *retrospectively* illumines the fury of the preceding climactic orchestral passage. I wonder if the juxtaposition of names — which was not Ravenscroft's or Auden's, but, I suspect, the composer's, as the coda emerges from the shape of the music rather than the text—made an immediate point in 1936. It is almost too subtly made, and yet how powerful it is provided that it is heard as a last ghastly comment on the preceding dance of death. It is the moment—and the song—where public impingement is most dramatically registered in the cycle, where public comment takes over from private statement. The two names that are extrapolated from the litany and placed in sequence and in isolation are the names of the hunter and the hunted—German, Jew:

Ex. 7

If anywhere, it was surely in the central songs of the cycle, and especially in 'Rats Away!' and 'Dance of Death', that Britten and Auden symbolically declared their political hand; and perhaps I should have mentioned earlier that clearly the 'Dance of Death' idea—the image—had its origins in Auden, whose *The Dance of Death* had been first performed in public by the Group Theatre in 1935. We may continue to wonder, as I have already wondered, how apparent the symbolism of *Our Hunting Fathers* was to the audience; how quick people were to catch the references and clues. We may be pretty sure, however, that the central songs spoke more clearly to the audience than the texts of the Prologue and Epilogue which are Auden at his most oblique and opaque.[33] They were the last sections of the work to be completed and in reverse order at that. John Fuller, in a commentary on Auden's Epilogue, concedes that 'It is an intellectual statement of some complexity', the obscurity of which 'makes it an odd choice as a text for music'. Mr Fuller, nonetheless, is able to tell us that the two stanzas are 'two views of love' and concludes that they contrast 'reason's collaboration with reason's modification, individualism with collectivism, Victorian *laissez-faire* with the Communist revolution'.[34] The analysis is a thoughtful one, and I do not do justice to it here. If I concentrate on Mr Fuller's last sentence, another kind of litany, it is not to mock it but simply to suggest that if it does represent a true list of contrasting contents, the probability of getting those abstract concepts over to an audience in the context and terms of music was a shade unrealistic, though as always Britten's actual setting of the words was exemplary in its clarity and sensitivity to nuance and rhythm. Against all one's expectations, in fact, the music does in a sense *clarify* the words, up to the point that is when one stops experiencing the music and asks oneself what the words actually mean. There the difficulty begins; still difficult for us and wholly baffling, I retrospectively guess, for the Norwich audience in 1936.

What seems to have seized Britten's imagination and feeling in the Epilogue is the idea of anonymity versus romantic individualism — he would have found the idea of the anonymous craftsman serving the community appealing (and indeed it was an idea to which he held to some degree throughout his life). It is not surprising then that it is this concept that Britten musicalizes, launching the word 'anonymous' on the wings of one of those extended melismas which are so conspicuous a feature of *Our Hunting Fathers* as a whole; and after that, a final reference to the first line of Auden's from which the work takes its title, and the epilogue to the Epilogue, for orchestra alone, a glacial, parodistic funeral march[35] (Mahler's influence again dominant) — a kind of spectral hunting music, a requiem for those who were danced, hunted, to death — which he had been scoring on one of those days when the news was particularly bad. It is certainly suggestive of the bleak future into which artists felt themselves borne on the tide of the thirties.

So *Our Hunting Fathers* comes to its disillusioned end—in some confusion, perhaps, because of Auden's private language. But the sense of commitment, of engagement, is profound and stirring, once one has decoded the work. And that it is not too specific, too topical, is surely one of its strengths, for the hunting, the hawking, the persecution, goes on in other places, other times; and death goes on dancing on other continents, in other decades, all the way from Belsen to Cambodia. To quote from Britten's diaries once more, 'What country will be in need of treatment now?' *Our Hunting Fathers* speaks to us still. Our awareness of the poet's and composer's awareness of the dark deeds done in Europe, and how that awareness was built into the fabric and structure of their song-cycle 'on Animals' is an essential part of our understanding of a work that does honour to its creators' compassion and conscience in 1936 as well as testifying to their great gifts.

Notes

1 Samuel Hynes, *The Auden Generation* (London: Faber & Faber, 1976).

2 Edward Mendelson, ed., *The English Auden (Poems, Essays and Dramatic Writings, 1927–1939)* (London: Faber & Faber, 1977), pp. 245–7.

3 Edward Mendelson points out that this disposition was also shared by Auden who '. . . for all his violent language of revolt in *The Orators* . . . remained the "Son of a nurse and doctor" who had absorbed their work-ethic and commitment to public service. He could no more retreat into bohemianism, or into an ironic contempt for his responsibilities, than he could retreat to the moon.' (Edward Mendelson, *Early Auden*, Chapter 6, 'Private Places' (London: Faber & Faber, 1981).)

4 Myfanwy Piper, *Death in Venice*, Libretto (based on the short story by Thomas Mann) (London: Faber Music, 1973), pp. 3, 22.

5 W. H. Auden and C. Day-Lewis, 'Preface', *Oxford Poetry 1927* (Oxford: Basil Blackwell, 1927), p. v.

6 *The Auden Generation*, p. 32.

7 In the case of Auden, Mendelson puts it thus: 'Now, more than at any other time, Auden is divided: between the public summons and the private wish. . . .' Professor Mendelson explores the dichotomy at length and in compelling detail (*Early Auden*, Chapter 9, 'The Great Divide').

8 *The Poet's Tongue*, An Anthology chosen by W. H. Auden and John Garrett (London: G. Bell & Sons Ltd, 1935).

9 'Psychology and Art To-day', in Geoffrey Grigson, ed., *The Arts To-day* (London: John Lane The Bodley Head, 1935), p. 20.

10 See *The Auden Generation*, p. 15.

11 See *The Auden Generation*, p. 169.

12 'Sir, no man's enemy, forgiving all', in *The English Auden*, p. 36.

13 *The Auden Generation*, p. 12.

14 '[Auden] had no doubts about the urgency of the times. . . . Yet the conventional portrait, so reassuringly naïve and symmetrical, of the young Auden setting out to conquer the double nemesis of fascism and neurosis is simpler than the truth. Like many young men of radical sympathies in revolutionary times, he was in fact not so much *engagé* as anxious to become *engagé*, and he was searching more for the will to act than for actions to perform.' (*Early Auden*, Chapter 9, 'The Great Divide'.)

15 In writing to *The Times* (23 November 1979) about the Blunt affair, Professor Eric Burhop sets out with admirable clarity the circumstances which compelled so many of the younger generation of intellectuals in the thirties to seek the political shelter to which I refer:

The great depression of the 1930s had eaten deep into the whole social fabric. Huge unemployment, malnutrition, the dole, means test, hunger marchers — these were the realities of the time. Clearly the conventional capitalist market economy had failed and it is not surprising that the brightest spirits in our universities were looking toward alternative social systems — some towards financial quirks like social credit, but many more toward Marxist solutions.

Earnest groups of young students, and by no means only students of economics, were discussing the labour theory of value, reading the classic works of Marx and Engels and their simplified, if superficial, popularisations such as John Strachey's *The Coming Struggle for Power*.

The Oxford Union resolution ['That this House will in no circumstances fight for its King and Country'] which caused such shivers to run down the spine of the Establishment, was one way of warning that a society which could not provide a minimum of opportunity or subsistence standards for very large numbers of its people was hardly worth defending. Naturally there was great interest in the Soviet Union, which was attempting to build a society based on a different, Marxist economic system.

The rise of Nazism was itself a direct result of the obvious insufficiency and worldwide collapse of the market economy. The persecution and exodus from Nazi Germany of many of the greatest intellectual figures of our time naturally had a maximum impact in our universities. Nazism appeared the most evil thing any of us had seen.

Our own Government, under Neville Chamberlain, seemed hell-bent on appeasing Hitler. The press and radio applauded Munich with almost the same unanimity and lack of historic analysis as they have exercised during the past few days in the Blunt affair. During the period between 1935 and August, 1939, the only force that stood staunchly against Nazism, and seemed capable of offering effective resistance to it and its aims in Spain, Austria and Czechoslovakia, was the Soviet Union and its Red Army.

16 Boys, the writer and teacher; Reeve, the son of the vicar of St John's Church, Lowestoft; Dunkeley and Barton were boyhood friends.

17 Flat 2, West Cottage Road, West End Green, London NW6.

18 The younger of Britten's two sisters, four years older than the composer.

19 Britten's brother, older by six years.

20 Marjorie was Robert Britten's first wife and John is his elder son.

21 Frank and Ethel Bridge lived at Friston in Sussex.

22 It is interesting that in an essay on 'Writing' that Auden contributed in 1932 to a children's encyclopedia, hunting and its practices are called in to clarify the argument about language that he is presenting. (See *Early Auden*, Chapter 1, 'The Exiled Word'.)

23 Benjamin Britten, *Paul Bunyan*, Op. 17, Vocal Score (London: Faber Music, 1978). The operetta was withdrawn in 1941 and revised in 1974.

24 W. H. Auden, *Paul Bunyan*, Libretto (London: Faber Music, 1976), p. 38.

25 Gordon Jacob, quoted in Michael Kennedy, *The Works of Ralph Vaughan Williams* (London: Oxford University Press,

1964), p. 164. Gordon Jacob studied at the Royal College of Music from 1919 to 1923.

26 Benjamin Britten, *Death in Venice*, Op. 88, Vocal Score (London: Faber Music, 1975), p. 167, fig. 198.

27 In the programme note that Britten wrote for the first performance at Norwich, he described the close of 'Rats Away!' in these words: 'At the end the wood-wind protest [i.e. the motto] dies away somewhat hopelessly. . . .', words which would seem to imply that the rats were indeed victorious. In a later programme note which Britten wrote for a revival of *Our Hunting Fathers* in 1950, he seemed to take a rather different view of how the contestants find themselves at the end of the song: 'The rodents reappear only to vanish with the restatement of the motto.' As I point out in n. 30 below, there is some reason to believe that the composer himself in the post-war years may have drifted out of touch with a work that belonged so emphatically to a period that he had put behind him, and may have had some difficulty in recollecting all the finer detail of the original symbolism.

28 In the programme of 25 September 1936 the names of the Festival's President and Vice-Presidents, the Members of the General Committee and Festival Guarantors are listed in full, along with their titles, decorations and other indications and designations of social role and status. The lists make absolutely clear that a large proportion of the Festival's supporters would scarcely have wished to 'guarantee' a work so subversive of established values and received opinion—of the world they lived in—as *Our Hunting Fathers*.

29 Peter Pears, 'The Vocal Music', in Donald Mitchell and Hans Keller, eds., *Benjamin Britten: A Commentary on His Works from a Group of Specialists* (London: Rockliff, 1952), p. 62. (Also: Greenwood Press reprint, U.S.A., 1972.)

30 Britten himself seems to have been confused about the roll-call of names in Ravenscroft's poem. In his note for the first performance in 1936 he writes: 'The soprano runs rapidly through the names of most of the birds concerned in this hunt'; and in general he does not lose sight of the fact that it is hawking, not fox-hunting, that is the ostensible topic of the 'Dance of Death'. But by 1950 Britten's memory seems to have blurred, and in his later note (see n. 27 above) he writes: 'The Dogs are called in groups . . . and with merry Folk-Song and Dance the kill is gleefully anticipated', a description which surely has more to do with fox-hunting than hawking. The erroneous references in fact are exceptionally interesting, suggesting as they do that what may have been upper-most in Britten's mind all along was the traditional form of hunt-ing — the one, by the way, with which his audience would have been presumed to be most familiar. The character of the musical invention also supports this view. It is fascinating to observe that Britten's 1936 note is absolutely devoid of any political references whatsoever; there is not so much as a hint of any political content. In the 1950 note, however, he does allow himself to draw the listener's attention to the juxtaposition of 'German' and 'Jew' in the litany of names, though he says no more than that. Did he imagine in 1936 that all the necessary connections and reactions would be made, without prompting from the authors? Or that those who were informed among the audience, and cared, would make the connections anyway — and that the rest should be abandoned to their complacent ignorance?

31 Benjamin Britten, *Our Hunting Fathers*, Op. 8, Pocket Score (London: Boosey & Hawkes, 1936), p. 44, fig. 36 – p. 49, fig. 42.

32 *Our Hunting Fathers*, Pocket Score, p. 61, fig. 49 – p. 73, fig. 58.

33 Since writing about Auden's Prologue and Epilogue, I have much benefited from reading Professor Mendelson's admirably clarifying exposition of these two texts. In the light of his commentary on the Epilogue (*Early Auden*, Chapter 10, 'The Insufficient Touch') I feel altogether less confident that 'baffling' is the right word to use about it as a poem; but as a *text for music* I think it continues to present special difficulties, and complexities. He also points out (in his Introduction) that 'free verse was, above all, *difficult*: difficult to write, difficult to read'; and the Prologue to *Our Hunting Fathers* seems to me to fall precisely into this category. (About this particular text Professor Mendelson writes in

Chapter 9, 'The Great Divide'.) He further and very interestingly observes of much the same period in Auden's verse that 'traditional stanzas are left mostly for satire, the regular verse standing as a rebuke to the irregularity and confusion into which the modern world has fallen'. This is certainly often true, though one may wonder whether the regularity of the Epilogue in fact does much to lessen the relative obscurity of the poem.

34 John Fuller, *A Reader's Guide to W. H. Auden* (London: Thames and Hudson, 1970), p. 101.

35 *Our Hunting Fathers*, Pocket Score, p. 84, fig. 65–end.

A very cold day - again

JANUARY, 1936.

Wednesday 15
(15-351)

Up early & get to Sho Square at 9.45. Some bother over parts of orchestra, but I eventually get down to Blackheath at 11.0 for big T.P.O. recording. A large orchestra for me — Fl. Ob. Bsn. Tpt. Harp (Marie Korchinska — very good), Vln, Vla. Vlc. CB. Percussion & wind machine — a splendid team. The music I wrote really comes off well — &, for what is wanted, creates quite a lot of sensation! The whole trouble, & what takes so much time is that over the music has to be spoken a verse — kind of patter — written by Auden — in strict rhythm with the music. To represent the train noises. Then is too much to be spoken in a single breath by the one voice (it is essential to keep to the same voice & to have no breaks) so we have to record separately — me, having to conduct both from an improvised visual metronome — flashes on the screen — a very difficult job! Legg speaks the stuff splendidly tho'. Recordings last from 11.0 — 2.30 - lunch — 3.15 — 5.30. So pretty dead. Bett & I prepare meal here — miss one — & after - much 'phoning (S 7. B. notably) & then work at Te Deum for a bit — too late tho' & not to bed till 12.0 — & it's so difficult to get up these mornings!

II. Sound-tracks

In my first lecture I quoted an evaluation of Britten by himself—
how he saw himself and his career at the beginning of 1936. On
that first page of his new diary he wrote:

> 1936 . . . finds me earning my living . . . at the G.P.O. film Unit
> under John Grierson and Cavalcanti, writing music and supervising
> sounds for films . . . at the rate of £5 per week, but . . . with the
> possibility of it being increased to £10 per week or £2 per day. . . .

Also employed there was the poet, W. H. Auden; indeed it was
through their joint work for the GPO Film Unit that Britten and
Auden came to meet.[1] It is to some of their work for films that I now
want to turn, and at the same time to consider the role that film,
and above all documentary film, played in the thirties, not only in
the productions of the GPO Film Unit but elsewhere. However, as
soon as one starts to think about the documentary movement, one
is drawn into a discussion of the importance allotted to education in
the thirties in many fields other than school or university.

The traditional belief in the value of education was powerfully
active, but with the added ingredient that the educative process
could lead also to a desirable scepticism about prevailing establishment values as inculcated and disseminated by prep school and
public school. However, prep school and public school, though
paradoxically they bred a whole generation of dissenters, were not
the places where one would first look for that 'change of heart'
which would encourage education to be an instrument of criticism
and social change rather than an agent of conformism. That had to
be achieved, if achieved at all, away from the classroom and the
playing fields; and in a singular way it was in the film studio in the
thirties that a certain subversion of establishment values began. It
was surely in a contrary, anti-establishment spirit that Paul Rotha,

the distinguished film director, whose work was a prominent
feature of the thirties, defined documentary film (with the accent
already on fact rather than fantasy) as an attempt 'to use cinema for
purposes more important than entertainment'.[2] And it was
precisely this educative purpose—the dissemination of facts, the
stimulation of civic responsibility, the countering of misleading, or
slanted, information from other influential sources—that was
among the principal aims of many of those associated with the
GPO Film Unit, even if they may have been less overtly committed
than was Rotha to propagandizing.

Although these ideas may have seemed radical and even extreme
at the time, were they not in fact very close to orthodox liberal
views? Persuasion by argument, by appeal to reason, by presenting
the 'facts'? Nothing very revolutionary here. In fact, all good,
sound educational principles. The innovatory difference, perhaps,
resided in the transfer of the power of disseminating information
from the private realm—from newspapers, say—to the public
domain, to an organization accountable to the public, through the
government department to which it was attached, and which was
presumed to have the public interest, not a private, commercial
interest, at heart. That was the radically new principle involved,
and it was indeed a remarkable institutional development.[3] But for
all that, it is plain that the thinking that went into it derived from
ideas about education, about the role of the educative process in the
formation of a well-ordered, well-informed community, which
would have been the intellectual property of the many liberal-
minded or 'progressive' schoolmasters and mistresses who, paradoxically enough, so often in the thirties taught in the private sector
(as Auden himself did).[4]

However, there were two sides to 'education' in the thirties: the
eccentric mythology of Auden and his friends, on the one hand—
about which I shall have more to say in my third lecture—and on
the other, what I have already pointed out: the general feeling
that educational advance would in particular improve the quality
of cultural life for the mass of the people. The spin-off here,
musically speaking, was the idea of 'music for the people', music of

quality (and therefore essentially non-commercial) that would 'speak' directly to performers and to audiences, and also have some social content. This was a typical thirties concept, part educational, part propagandist, and was certainly one with which Britten felt in sympathy; principles moreover which in a general way he was practising in his work with the GPO Film Unit, the Group Theatre, and so on. How active and prolific Britten was in film-making has, I think, not been sufficiently realized. It is an illumination I owe to his diaries, in which John Grierson and Paul Rotha are two names that frequently recur. Grierson, who was the head of the GPO Film Unit—formerly part of the Empire Marketing Board, and then set up as the information branch of the General Post Office in 1933—was the father of the documentary; and 'education', when he was expounding the principles of documentary film, was often on his lips:

. . . the documentary idea was not basically a film idea at all, and the film treatment it inspired only an incidental aspect of it. The medium happened to be the most convenient and most exciting available to us. The idea itself, on the other hand, was a new idea for public education: its underlying concept that the world was in a phase of drastic change affecting every manner of thought and practice, and the public comprehension of the nature of that change vital. There it is, exploratory, experimental and stumbling, in the films themselves: from the dramatization of the workman and his daily work to the dramatization of modern organization and the new corporate elements in society to the dramatization of social problems: each a step in the attempt to understand the stubborn raw material of our modern citizenship and wake the heart and the will to their mastery. Where we stopped short was that, with equal deliberation, we refused to specify what political agency should carry out that will or associate ourselves with any one of them. Our job specifically was to wake the heart and the will: it was for the political parties to make before the people their own case for leadership. [5]

That characteristic statement certainly supports what Grierson said of himself: 'I look on cinema as a pulpit and use it as a propagandist.'[6]

No less important a figure was Paul Rotha, happily still alive today, whose book *Documentary Film* was published in 1936, by Faber & Faber. (Here perhaps I might be permitted a publisher's parenthesis: Faber & Faber led the field in the publication of many of the principal poets, dramatists, architects and film-makers of the thirties, to such an extent indeed that Faber & Faber itself might be regarded as part of the thirties phenomenon. In some ways this was a surprising development since the political views of the writers in many instances must have run directly counter to the political beliefs of T. S. Eliot, the dominant literary influence at Faber & Faber during this period, and of Geoffrey Faber, the founder of the firm.)

It was with Paul Rotha—I think a more politically minded film-maker than Grierson—that Britten was to collaborate in this same year, 1936, on the so-called 'Peace Film' (its title was in fact *Peace of Britain*) which was to become the centre of a controversy. Although Rotha was perhaps more radical than Grierson in his politics, he too was a vigorous proponent of the educative potentialities of the documentary film:

> . . . it is absurd to suggest that cinema, with its powers to enlarge the public's social conscience, to create new standards of culture, to stir mental apathies, to build new understandings and, by virtues inherent in its form, to become the most powerful of all modern preachers — it is absurd to suggest that it can be left in the hands of commercial speculators to be used as a vehicle for purposeless fictional stories. There must be a world outside that represented by the entertainment film. There must be sources of production other than those demanding only profit. There must be kinds of cinema and ends to serve other than those which portray an artificial world conceived under mass-production methods at the dictates of the balance-sheet. There is—the world of propaganda and education.

Real and creative thought must be about real things. Let cinema explore outside the limits of what we are told constitutes entertainment. Let cinema attempt the dramatisation of the living scene and the living theme, springing from the living present instead of from the synthetic fabrication of the studio. Let cinema attempt film interpretations of modern problems and events, of things as they really are today, and by so doing perform a definite function. Let cinema recognise the existence of real men and women, real things and real issues, and by so doing offer to State, Industry, Commerce, to public and private organisations of all kinds, a method of communication and propaganda to project not just personal opinions but arguments for a world of common interests.

. . . the cinema has at last become alive outside the limits of the studio balance sheet. It has found temporary salvation in serving the ends of education and persuasion. It has found fresh air beyond the sound-and-idea-proof studios in what Grierson has called the 'creative treatment of actuality'.[7] And among these new forms, somewhat beyond the simple descriptive terms of the teaching film, more imaginative and expressive than the specific publicity picture, deeper in meaning and more skilful in style than the news-reel, wider in observation than the travel picture or lecture film, more profound in implication and reference than the plain 'interest' picture, there lies Documentary. And the documentary method may well be described as the birth of creative cinema.[8]

Those statements by Grierson and Rotha show very clearly the kind of ideas circulating at the time among those working for the GPO Film Unit and similar organizations, ideas which not only influenced Britten but also must have made a particular appeal to him. The idea of encouraging 'civic participation', above all the powerful moralizing and educative motives which gave rise to the group's activities and constituted its particular ethic—with these aspects of the unit Britten would have found himself in real sympathy. On top of that, here was an agency of government working for the public good, for the betterment of public information, by the imaginative dissemination of news about the public services and the ideals which promoted them through the hitherto unexploited medium of film; and not just film, but *documentary* film, which as we have already seen from the texts by Grierson and Rotha was in itself a brand of film-making peculiarly associated with the thirties. Indeed I think it is important to assert at this stage that documentary film, which attracted to it the brilliant talents who, through the exercise of their gifts, realized the medium's potentialities and thus endowed it with its historical significance, was one of the forms, one of the media, created by the thirties, and which functioned in a highly original way as a vehicle for those ideas and ideals that we may recognize as demonstrably of the period. In short, one of the thirties art-forms—if the paradox may be forgiven—was the documentary, the (in some respects) *anti*-art film.

The documentary dimension was not, of course, confined to film but was virtually a generally accepted mode of approach, almost a unifying style. Its influence on the other media was pervasive. Perhaps the only comparable activity in our own day would be those television programmes that sustain and extend the documentary tradition from the thirties—another interesting example of the post-war influence exerted by the period. But alas, despite the vast expansion of technological resources, television has generated nothing like the intellectual excitement of the public service film concept in the thirties, nor has it drawn to it creators of the calibre of Auden and Britten, Grierson and Rotha. The spirit of adventure, of genuine experimentation, has declined seemingly in strict relation to the sophistication of the technology involved and the notion of the mass medium. At the very centre of the activity surrounding the creation of this exciting new form in the thirties, and the development of the new techniques required to exploit it, was Benjamin Britten, the GPO Film Unit's resident composer and sound-track supervisor.

I have already mentioned the built-in tension that was part of

Britten's relationship to the politics of his time, the generating source of which was his pacifism. An opportunity now occurred for him to participate in a venture that was designed, amid the gathering clamour of preparations for war, to argue the cause — and also a logical case — for peace. Interestingly enough, it took the shape of a short documentary film, the 'Peace Film', made by Paul Rotha for Strand Films. It makes its first appearance in Britten's diary on 12 March. He had spent the earlier part of the day on GPO Film Unit work, discussing the music he had to write for a new film—'A rather lovely thing about English villages'⁹—with Marion Grierson, John Grierson's sister. But later he went 'on to Strand films to talk to Paul Rotha about a short film on peace which has been hurriedly commissioned by T.U.C. & League of Nations Union'.

It is of course of very great interest that this pacific counter–argument should have been conceived as a *film*—it tells us something about how film, as a means of information, of education, of persuasion, was regarded in the thirties. It was, I think, thought of as the propaganda vehicle *par excellence* and Rotha himself, as we have learned, had a committed view of film as propaganda, and political propaganda at that. This was a policy that the GPO Film Unit, with its official status, would not have been able to countenance. Thus if a 'Peace Film' were to be made, it had to be done by an independent group: hence Strand Films. Clearly though, Britten's reputation as a composer for film and perhaps also as a phenomenally fast worker, was such that it was natural to approach him for the music, and in addition his own strongly held pacifist opinions, widely known among his friends and working colleagues, must have made him the most appropriately qualified collaborator.

Britten writes that it was the TUC that shared in the commissioning of the film. I am not sure that TUC support was quite as official as that. Paul Rotha, who has written a detailed account of the whole 'Peace Film' affair in his *Documentary Diary*,¹⁰ makes it clear that support came mostly from private sources—from, among others, Stafford Cripps, George Cadbury, and D. N. Pritt—

although the approach to Cripps, who then enlisted the aid of friends and sympathizers, was made by J. J. Taylor, the political secretary of the Transport and General Workers' Union. So, while the TUC interest in the enterprise may not have been an official one, the connections through the personalities Rotha mentions were very close, and suggest how deeply entrenched in 1936, in some left-wing circles, was support for the League of Nations, for anti-rearmament, for a pacific—if not strictly pacifist—policy.

Britten had first talked with Rotha on 12 March. On the 17th: 'Spend all the day in Hampstead working on peace film music. Being entirely out of mood do some pretty poor stuff I'm afraid.' On the 18th: 'Finish film music in the morning'; on the 19th: 'Touch up as far as possible Film music'; and next day, the 20th: 'Up to Wardour St. to see Rotha & his new peace film at 1.0'. In the afternoon Britten picked up the parts from the copyist and next morning, the 21st: 'Up early & to Wardour St.—Imperial Sound Studios at 9.0 to record my music for this L.N.U. & T.U.C. peace film—directed by Rotha; an orchestra of 10[11]—quite good. It goes quite well, tho' it is a job to fit it in.'

This last reference is to the technical process of matching with music of the precise duration those sections of the film of which music formed an integral part. When Britten was writing for films, the process of composition and recording was conducted in three distinct stages. There was first the discussion of the film with the director, script-writer, sponsors, and so on, after which no doubt the first musical ideas would be conceived. Second, the composer would have been shown a rough-cut of the film, from which he would have taken away pretty precise information of the scenes or incidents for which music was required and, even more important, timings, i.e. the required durations at which he was to write. Third, the music would be recorded on the sound-track. There would then follow the most critical stage of all, the final editing of the film and synchronization of the sound-track; and it was precisely at this vital point that Britten's skills in the cutting-room were so greatly valued and widely acknowledged. Because it could happen — and indeed did happen in the case of *Night Mail*, as Basil Wright recalls — that, however meticulous and careful was the completion of the third stage, of the recording, the sound-track could prove to offer an imperfect 'fit'. A sound-track too long by so many feet (as in the case of *Night Mail*) was the kind of problem that might materialize at the last moment. It was the speed and skill that Britten brought to the tailoring of the sound-track, the editing of his score, in its already recorded form, that won the admiration of his colleagues in the GPO Film Unit and elsewhere.

So the 'Peace Film' was a job—one in which we may presume Britten had his heart, whatever his momentary doubts about the quality of his score—that was composed and recorded all within the space of five days, an indication of the kind of professional skill he was able to deploy in the film studio at the age of twenty-two. There was, it seems, only one hitch in the whole operation and that cropped up a few days later, but it seems to have been swiftly dealt with, for at 5 p.m. on the 24th, he was obviously in a position to see the film for the first time with his music *in situ*: '[it] has come off excellently', writes Britten, 'except for the final chorus — & it needs some subtle wangling to get over that.'

Peace of Britain is a very short film, undeniably of its time and now—undeniably—a period piece. And yet the fact that it still speaks to us compellingly, as I believe it does, is surely evidence of the enduring power of its visual·images and the skill of the editing; and though the captions and commentary are of the simplest, deliberately so, nonetheless they are cunningly designed to appeal to the widest spectrum of public opinion. The 'Peace Film' was, I suppose, the equivalent of a political poster, but a thousand times more effective because it could rely for its few minutes' duration on a captive audience. The music was relatively minimal, but it is appropriately menacing (weapons, aerial bombardment) or affirmative and uplifting (support the League, opt for peace not war) and always energetic, helping—despite the very slender means—to make the film's point that if peace is to be achieved something active has to be done about it ('Write to your MP'). An effective, crisp little score within the constraints imposed on it by time and limited resources. Britten seems to have had something more

ambitious in mind for the close of the film — if not, then the
reference to a 'chorus' in his diary is puzzling. [12] It is my guess that
the technical difficulties to which he referred proved insuperable
and the chorus was omitted.

I think we would all agree, whatever opinions we might hold
about the merits of the film, that it would be hard to think of it as
dangerous, subversive or revolutionary; and yet by an extraordinary
stroke of irony, Rotha's 'Peace Film' sparked off a sharp political
controversy, which suddenly and unexpectedly erupted in the
national press and was faithfully documented in his diary by a
gratified composer:

> 8 APRIL:
> The fuss caused by the Censor not passing that little Rotha Peace
> film is colossal. ½ centre pages of Herald & News Chronicle, &
> Manchester Guardian — BBC. News twice. Never has a film had
> such good publicity!

It was undoubtedly good publicity for the film, though less so for
the composer: in the long *Manchester Guardian* account of the
affair Britten's name was not mentioned. [13] Of course it is difficult at
this distance in time to distinguish the motive behind the attempted
censorship—it is clear I think that bringing into play the question
of a breach of War Office copyright (it all hung on the shots of a
tank) was wholly make-believe. It was surely a typically bungling
establishment way of going about the suppression of an unwelcome
'subversive' opinion—I do not find anything to be surprised about
in that. Much more interesting in my view is the probability that
the move to ban the little and, as it must seem to us now, innocuous
Peace of Britain had its roots in authority's fear of the influence the
film might have on public opinion through it being widely shown
in news theatres and cinemas round the country—a vastly inflated
fear, I am sure, but one that testifies to the influential status of
cinemas and news theatres in the thirties as disseminators of topical
news, comment and information. The statistics Rotha gives are
indeed impressive and perhaps with these figures in mind the
attempt at censorship makes more sense. For example, he writes

that 'over Easter, 30 copies of the film were showing in London alone', while orders for copies were received from overseas. It is an ironic reflection that at least part of this flurry of interest had been aroused by the attempt to keep the film off the screen. [14]

The effort to stop or impede the distribution of the film, no doubt because of the weakness of the case and the fuss made in the liberal press, collapsed—seemingly overnight; for the very next day, on 9 April 1936, we find our composer seated with a friend in a news theatre in London: 'See the now 'famous' Peace Film', he remarks laconically in his diary.

The character of the music for *Peace of Britain* indicates that Britten was an activist for peace; and there is yet another little-known and now all but forgotten musical document that shows him active again — the same cause, but this time marching for peace. *Pacifist March* (see pp. 68–9) belongs in fact to the early months of 1937. It was written for the Peace Pledge Union [15] and the words were by Ronald Duncan, who at a much later stage was to be the librettist of Britten's first chamber opera, *The Rape of Lucretia*. We might now think that Duncan's somewhat militant pacifist spirit and Britten's wellnigh military march strike an ironic note, but certainly any irony was unintentional.

The music—like the music for *Peace of Britain*, activist in character—was clearly influenced by models (Brecht, Eisler) of political propaganda songs, proletarian marching songs and the like, current in Europe at the time. Britten's example is certainly written with characteristic ingenuity: the simplest of musical ideas that could be mastered by a musically untutored group, ideas that could readily be memorized and that were also, once heard, not easily forgotten. The refrain in particular sticks in the mind, as no doubt was the composer's intention.

The *Pacifist March* of 1937 would scarcely prepare us for the *War Requiem* of 1961, but these pacifist affirmations from the thirties, in film and song, marked the beginning of that noble anti-militaristic strand in Britten's art. When we return, as we do now, to 1936, it is

PACIFIST MARCH

Voice Part only
PRICE 1ᵈ

Words by
RONALD DUNCAN

Music by
BENJAMIN BRITTEN

bit-ter-ness have been used in   paint - ing our his-to-ry,   That's been
wear-i-ness we have wait - ed   in queues of un-ea-sy length,   For the
tender-ness have been slaked and   torn by high ex - plos - ives,   Pet - rol
laz - i-ness strive and strug - gle,   mud - dle and fum - ble   T'wards

smudg'd with the stain of   war.   Em - pire we've sto - len,
dole   or the cin - e - ma. Though Means Test   in - sults,
pump and the tin fruit   sign.   We've tol - er - a - ted,
peace or for-get - ful - ness.   Cen - tu-ries of suf-fer-ing,

swol-len,   Our im - pe - ri - al greed for   more.
as-saults,   Our   cul - ture, na - tive   dig - ni - ty.
paint-ed,   Cor - ru - ga - ted iron for our   roof.
shuffling,   Years re - vol - ving and   re - sol - ving.

Published by
THE PEACE PLEDGE UNION
96 Regent Street, London. W. 1

H. 14717

4   The printed song sheet of *Pacifist March*

2

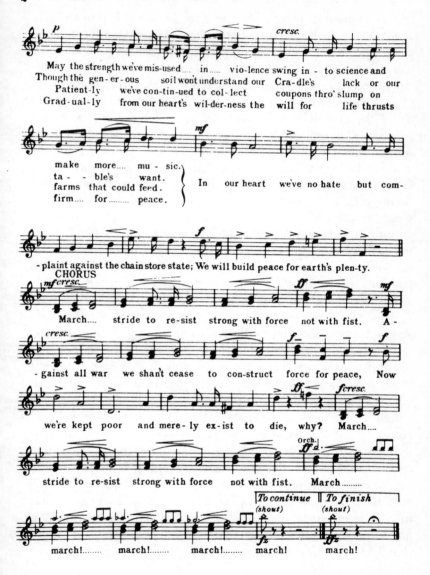

May the strength we've mis-used.... in..... vio-lence swing in - to science and
Though the gen - er - ous soil won't understand our Cra - dle's lack or our
Patient-ly we've con-tin-ued to col-lect coupons thro' slump on
Grad-ual-ly from our heart's wil-der-ness the will for life thrusts

make more.... mu - sic.)
ta - - ble's want.
farms that could feed. } In our heart we've no hate but com-
firm.... for........ peace.

- plaint against the chain store state; We will build peace for earth's plen-ty.

CHORUS

March.... stride to re-sist strong with force not with fist. A-

- gainst all war we shan't cease to con-struct force for peace, Now

we're kept poor and mere-ly ex-ist to die, why? March....

stride to re-sist strong with force not with fist. March........

To continue ‖ *To finish*
(shout) (shout)

march!........ march!........ march!........ march! march!

in fact to another march, this time for brass band, though once
again it is a work bound up with the particular political events of the
year. The march for band, eventually called *Russian Funeral*,[16]
was conceived and completed in a phenomenally short time:
Britten was thinking about how he might shape it on the afternoon
of 24 February, finished a first complete sketch before dinner on
the 27th, and delivered a fair full score for the copyist to his
publishers, Boosey & Hawkes, before lunch on 2 March. It was a
semi-political work written for a semi-political occasion, a concert
given at the Westminster Theatre, London, by the London Labour
Choral Union conducted by Alan Bush on Sunday, 8 March. I say
'semi-political' in connection with Britten's work because, or so it
seems to me, there was always a necessary ambiguity about his
commitment to anti-Fascist politics in the thirties. By that I do not
mean that his politics lacked conviction, sincerity or courage. But
the joker in the pack, if one may so describe it, was his stubborn
pacifism: he would go so far in opposing Fascism but certainly
would not, could not, participate in or condone violence and war.

This is an absolutely essential factor which we have to take into
account when considering Britten's relationship to the left-wing
movement, the anti-Fascist front, in England in the thirties. His
pacifism was a very powerful conviction indeed and it must, I
think, have meant that he was always marked out as one apart, even
when working within a group with the general political ideals of
which he was in close sympathy.[17] This divergence from the total
commitment of those who, honourably enough, were convinced
that Fascism must be opposed ultimately by armed force, and
agitated to that end, this other commitment of Britten's—which
was to have such profound and long-term consequences for his
art—must have isolated him a little from friends and colleagues. It is
utterly characteristic that his *Russian Funeral* juxtaposed not War
and *Glory* but War and *Death*. Indeed it was as 'War and Death'
that Britten described his march when it was first performed, at the
Westminster Theatre, on Sunday, 8 March 1936:

> To West. Theatre for London Labour Choral Soc. show of

Expedient (Brecht & Eisler) which is done with fine spirit under
Alan Bush. There are many fine things in this work, & it is splendidly dramatic—tho' use of chorus is not too satisfactory. The first
½ of programme was my 'War & Death'—during the show of which
I suffer more exquisite agony than ever before owing to uncertainty
of playing. I certainly have been a bit tactless in giving so thin a
texture for nervous players!

The reference to Brecht and Eisler is particularly interesting.[18]
There can be little doubt that the work of the politically committed
poet and composer from Germany—and not only Hanns Eisler's
music for Brecht but also Kurt Weill's—would have been of
particular interest to Britten and his friends and theatrical collaborators, an interest that, fascinatingly, was reciprocated: when in
1937 Brecht was drawing up a list of people in the theatre, some of
them outside Germany, with a view to the pooling of 'methods,
knowledge and experience', it included the names of W. H.
Auden, Christopher Isherwood and Rupert Doone—the director
of the Group Theatre.[19]

There is more that must be said about *Russian Funeral*: 'War
and Death'—Britten's only brass band piece—on the occasion of
its première a few days later. Perhaps it is of some relevance to
mention in this context the pronounced influence on it of a
contemporary Russian master, Shostakovich, whom Britten much
admired and was to go on admiring throughout his lifetime. He had
been playing through Shostakovich's Piano Concerto[20] with a
friend at the very time he was thinking about his *Russian Funeral*.
It is hard to imagine that Shostakovich was not in a very real sense a
model, and in the particular circumstances in which Britten found
himself—the obligation to complete a work in a few days—a
useful and inspiring one. Inspiring, I suggest, for a reason other
than the fact that from a purely musical point of view Shostakovich
enjoyed Britten's esteem. He would also have been esteemed
because he was Russian. I think we have to remind ourselves here
that in these dark days of the thirties, Russia and the Revolution
represented for many of the artists and intellectuals who crowd
these pages a peculiarly bright light, even a moral beacon, among

the expediencies and betrayals of decadent Western, that is to say capitalist, politics. I have no doubt that for Britten too this meant that contemporary Russian music had a significance, or at least an interest, over and above its quality as music. It was fortunate of course that Shostakovich was indisputably a man of brilliant talent, something to which Britten, obviously, would scarcely have been indifferent. But there would have been this extra element of excitement in the air about music that was inspired *and* Russian, or Soviet, in origin. For one thing, and especially for a musician, here was an area in which and about which it was possible to feel and to express optimism, a sentiment proper to youth, that otherwise had remarkably little opportunity to counter the prevailing pessimism of the period. We know now, or so I believe, how illusory that shining image of Russia was, not least in relation to the Spanish Civil War. It is surely the particular disillusionment in the arena of Spanish politics that makes Auden's view of the decade so telling. But when Britten was engaged on his march, there was no knowledge of any sordid intrigue to qualify or modify the idealism he shared with his circle.

There is perhaps one final point to be made about Russian influences on *Russian Funeral*. It was a characteristic of Britten as an artist—part of his 'realism', an aspect of his creative character to which I find myself returning again and again—that he took great care over matters of authenticity when composing a work that had quite clearly spelt-out associations or was tailor-made for a particular event. Thus he would have thought it very odd if his Russian march did not declare its 'Russian-ness' in some specific and identifiable way, not just in a general evocation of Russian atmosphere. It is not surprising then to find that *Russian Funeral* was in fact based on an authentic Russian funeral march tune. The wheel turns full circle when we learn further that it was a tune that Shostakovich was to use in 1957 as a main theme in the third movement of his Eleventh Symphony. By the strangest of coincidences, what a Soviet student of Shostakovich writes about this particular theme and this particular movement in the symphony precisely describes something of what the youthful Britten had in mind when composing *his* funeral march in 1936:

> The main theme of the third movement is a famous funeral song
> that the Russian proletariat sang in farewell to revolutionary
> fighters who had fallen in the struggle. The words are worthy of
> note. They glorify those who died in the struggle for the life,
> happiness and liberty of the people, those who, in their great love
> for the people, gave up their all, even life itself. [21]

The embracing of a model, Shostakovich, and the use of an
authentic Russian tune: these were part of Britten's composing
process, part of the 'realism', the guarantee of authenticity. It is the
'famous funeral song'—Death—that frames the quick middle
section—War; which means that the Death section, on its
recapitulation, is also heard to be the consequence of War, a simple
but striking, formal dramatic scheme, and one that must have
gratified the realistically minded pacifist composer.

Among all the influences that went into the making of what was,
in effect, a short symphonic poem for brass band, is that of Mahler,
who looms large in the slow funeral march section, and is especially present in Britten's soloistic instrumental writing. Small
wonder that his 'nervous players' felt so unprotected.

It is not surprising that during these months of 1936, even during
the few days in February when Britten was hard at work on his
Russian march—perhaps indeed just because he would have been
particularly aware at this time of political events—his diary
contains more than one anxious reference to the political issues of
the day, to war, death, Mussolini, armaments and Stanley
Baldwin. For example, on 29 February, he wrote:

> After dinner read a lot more 'Farewell to Arms' [Hemingway's
> novel], I think it is very exciting, tho' very terrible. Also listen to
> wireless, & hear that the Abyssinians are being routed by the Italians.
> How can we sit still, quibbling about sanctions — drivelling over
> increased armaments — being afraid to lose 2d on oil payments, yet
> being willing to spend £3000,000,000 on men-slaughtering
> machines — beats me. Yet the country detests this war, & says so —
> vide Hoare–Laval peace plan — but still <u>trusts</u> Baldwin and his dear
> government.

5 Two pages from Britten's MS full score of *Russian Funeral*
© The Britten Estate

9.

On 7 March, the day before the first performance of *Russian Funeral*, world issues again force themselves into Britten's diary:

> The international situation now is ludicrously complicated—Germany now discards Locarno & Versailles & occupies Rhine territory—Italian successes on Abyssinian front continue in spite of financial difficulties—Japan owing to the shooting of her statesmen in last week's revolt is more militaristic than ever—& Russia is pressed on the other side as well by Germany & Poland. Central Europe is a hot-bed of intrigue—and our re-armament plans mount up & up—etc. etc.!!!!

That was how the world looked to one young man on 7 March 1936, writing his diary at the end of the day. Not a bad précis, one might think, of how things stood; and moreover made not in autobiographical retrospect, after due meditation, but on the spot.

Although it is clear from these diary excerpts how politics impinged on a highly sensitive and aware young artist in 1936, it would be highly misleading to conclude that politics were all. They were not, as Britten's diaries also make perfectly clear. His personal life, family, obligations, his career, his performing, and what one can only guess to have been unceasing mental activity, the exercise of his prodigious musical imagination—there were a hundred and one other things besides politics to claim his attention and demand expenditure of energy, above all the sheer physical business of getting down on paper the notes that had been commissioned or that he wanted to write. Selective quotations can distort the true picture, as would certainly be the case if we relied solely on those political quotations and related them to the 'War and Death' performance at the Westminster Theatre, and added in for good measure that on that very day—8 March—even before the performance of *Russian Funeral* had taken place, Britten, so his diary tells us, was reading '[Montagu] Slater's new play—"Stay down miner" for deciding about music for it'. Slater, who was to be the librettist of *Peter Grimes* some nine years later, was in 1936 a vigorous left-wing novelist, poet and dramatist; and as the title of his new play suggests, which was a production of the Left Theatre group, an active and combative propagandist.[22]

The nature of these preoccupations might encourage us to believe that Britten was a kind of politico-musical activist; but the complete diary entries modify that impression, sometimes very amusingly and touchingly. For example, on the afternoon of 7 March, after the rehearsal of 'War and Death', other things and different experiences and distinctly non-political people intervened. For instance there was Mum—Mrs Britten—arriving from Suffolk to attend the performance next day to be met at Liverpool Street; there was a piano trio by Frank Bridge to rehearse with Bernard and Irene Richards in the afternoon;[23] and after supper, there was an outing, a treat:

> . . . we [Britten, his mother, and his sister, Barbara] go off to Carlton [cinema], where Mum is extravagant & pays 6/- each for us to see Harold Lloyd in Milky Way—a very amusing & well made comedy—not subtle of course but in spite of some slack & slow moments, very effective.

And then there was a bonus in the programme, which clearly gave the young composer pleasure and must have pleased his mother too:

> Also our 'Night Mail' is put on — & it goes down excellently with the Audience.

To Night Mail we shall come later; but first, Britten's mother — his Mum: it is impossible not to speculate a little about her feelings about her remarkable son. His gifts, though perhaps a shade alarming, can only have made her proud, like any mother. But she was the widow of a highly respected Lowestoft dental surgeon, and the kind of society and social life which surrounded her in Suffolk, and indeed had surrounded the family of which Britten was a member, could scarcely have prepared her for a son who, whatever his gifts, was to emerge as a brilliant and engaged participator in the left-wing London theatre. One cannot help wondering what Mrs Britten made of 'War and Death', of the ambience of the London

Labour Choral Union, and the propagandist Brecht-Eisler half of the programme, a wonderment that is intensified when we read Britten's diary for the next day — Sunday, the day of the première:

> Breakfast about 10.0 — Mum cooks it, & goes off to a Christian S. [Science] service at 11.30.

A memorable Sunday this: in the morning, Mary Baker Eddy whose Christian Science attracted so many middle and upper-class ladies in the twenties and thirties that it constituted a social phenomenon in its own right[24]—and 'War and Death' and Brecht-Eisler in the evening; and all the time Britten turning over *Stay down miner* in his mind. We are unlikely to know what Mum really made of it all. But a bare recital of the facts gives at least some indication of the texture of Britten's daily life. His diaries most valuably remind us of what in fact, as distinct from fiction (or theory), an artist's life is made—what feeds into it. Perhaps it is only politicians who actually live politics. (Perhaps that is what is wrong with politicians.) In any event, although music was always at the centre of Britten's life, he was never so preoccupied as to be able to allow himself to ignore the great issues of the day.

There was no escaping politics in the month of March, and the diaries accurately reflect what was now seen to be the growing menace of National Socialism in Germany. At home there was a new king, Edward VIII, on the throne, and Britten had expectations that a broadcast he made on 1 March might not be the usual text composed of royal platitudes — Britten was clearly influenced in these hopes by Edward's 'liberal' image. But disillusion ensued:

> The King . . . makes a speech to the 'Empire'. I had hoped that he would at least say something interesting—feeling that he is more of a personality than his father—something about the foreign situation or the League of Nations—but I was very disappointed.

It was not what Edward VIII thought about the League that counted. The reality was located elsewhere, in Germany in particular, and made itself felt in a variety of ways, for example in the news theatre, the forerunner of today's television news. Britten often dropped into a news theatre and on 12 March found there 'the German situation & our own [?self-] satisfied incompetence . . . made sickeningly real'. He made the visit in the company of a German acquaintance, Rudolph Holzmann ('back from Germany—he has had difficulty in getting permission to land') who later, on 24 March, gave Britten his personal impressions of what was happening in his native land:

> . . . back here for dinner at 7.30 to which Rudolph Holzmann comes. Talk music & politics chiefly—he is a bright & intelligent person & thoroughly musical. His account of present-day Germany is as depressing as possible. Now of course everyone is hanging on Hitler's lips for his answer to the League proposals. I suppose he will accept & that will postpone war for a year or so.

But Britten supposed wrongly, and the very next day, scribbled in a hectic hand at the top of the page, over the date 25 March, we read: 'Germany says—no—to proposals. How do we hedge now?' The hedging was yet to continue for a year or two; but the omens of war, gradually but inexorably, were becoming ever clearer.

Politics and personal life apart, there is another highly significant impression left by the diaries: the importance of the cultural, educative role of radio—of the BBC—in the thirties; especially of course in the field of music, but in other fields as well. One sees very clearly from documents like Britten's diaries just how substantial an agent of information the BBC was in this period. It not only provided the youthful Britten and those others of his generation with similar tastes and interests with opportunities to hear contemporary works which made infrequent appearances on concert programmes, not to speak of the classical repertoire, but also stood for the kind of achievement that an enlightened public service could, at its best, provide; and undoubtedly the GPO Film Unit reflected in some measure the kind of excellence promoted by the BBC. The film unit may have been more adventurous and radical in spirit — or drawn more radical spirits to it — but it was essentially part of the same constellation of liberal ideas that generated the philosophy of the BBC. Moreover, if Britten in some sense owed part of his education to the BBC, he must also, as a very attentive listener, have become thoroughly familiar with the potentialities and possibilities of radio, which stood him in good stead when he himself became pioneeringly involved in the making of radio features, of 'documentary' programmes.

The radio feature was an innovation for which the BBC was famous in the thirties. It was very close indeed to the concept and ideology of the documentary film, and, while bearing in mind that only sound was involved, one might claim that Grierson's succinct description of documentary film—'the creative treatment of actuality'—could equally well serve as a description of the documentary radio programme. The radio feature demands recognition as one of the principal new creative forms generated by the thirties, having its roots in specifically thirties ideas about social utility, the dissemination of information, the importance of educating ourselves about ourselves, and so on. It is easy to see how the radio feature, like the documentary film, sits very naturally in such a context. Incidentally, it is interesting to observe that both the radio feature and the documentary film were composite, mixed media, both making use of comparatively new and rapidly evolving technologies — the equivalent in some respects of the present-day relationship between the arts and electronics. Of this new medium too, Britten was one of the early makers; and when we come to the third medium, theatre, we shall find likewise that he was no less of a pioneer. It is an exceptional record.

But it was to the film studio that Britten first brought his gifts which were so happily in tune with the new developments in sound in the cinema industry and with the expertise of Alberto Cavalcanti at the GPO Film Unit, for whom sound was a special province and responsibility. And there was *Night Mail*, the history of which we can follow in Britten's diaries:

3 JANUARY:
Go up to Soho Square in morning for more discussions as to G.P.O. Sound. Now to complicate matters the Producer (Wright) can't

make suspicious Watt (director) see the point of Auden's lovely verse. So we make in the afternoon at Blackheath a rough 'take' of the verse alone (spoken by [Stuart] Legg) to cut the film roughly to, first. I go to see Ralph Hawkes [Britten's publisher] to put a cap on the discussions on my agreement with him & also to Whiteleys [the department store] for a hair cut.

4 JANUARY:
They still are fighting over the sound of G.P.O. so after telephone calls I fix not to go to the Unit today. So after shopping with Beth, have long practice at pft. & then go on with my arrangement of Rossini Suite [the *Soirées Musicales*, Op. 9] for Boosey & Hawkes.

On 6 January work continues on *Night Mail*:

To Soho Square by 10.0 where I meet Wright & Cavalcanti — after much delay down to studio at Blackheath in Wright's car. Then we cut in the test-bands for G.P.O. Spend whole day until 6.45 there. Back here late for dinner, after which write a lot of overdue letters — & a little gramophone before bath & bed.

7 JANUARY:
Another Blackheath day . . . Basil Wright takes Cavalcanti & me down by car & we spend all day on G.P.O. . . . Very interesting — but annoying that the music will have to be rushed owing to this delay. Also help Auden about one or two things with his film (Calendar of the Year).[25]

8 JANUARY:
I go to Blackheath with Wright & Cavalcanti all morning — at last get instructions for G.P.O. sound.

The next day, 9 January, was partly spent 'working at G.P.O. sound—train noises. Not very good as music—but I think that with the visuals they will be all right—one cannot write "music" to these minute instructions, when even the speed of the beat and number of bars is fixed. . . .'

The particular passage (see p. 82) that represents a steam engine accumulating energy and its pistons beginning to drive the wheels is scored for an ensemble drawn from a percussion group of a most

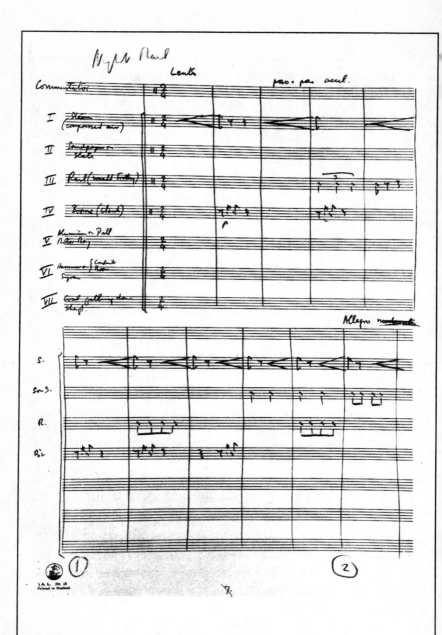

6 A page from Britten's MS full score of *Night Mail* © The Britten Estate

unorthodox constitution:

I	Steam (compressed air)
II	Sandpaper on slate
III	Rail (small trolley)
IV	Booms (clank)

V { Aluminium on Drill
    { Motor Moy [a hand-cranked, chain-operated camera]

VI { Hammer on $\frac{\text{Conduit}}{\text{Boom}}$
    { Syren

VII   Coal falling down shaft

One might well be forgiven for thinking that this was an 'orchestra' closer to, say, the sound-world of Varèse than Britten; and it is of course fascinating that here we find our youthful composer in 1936 imagining a kind of *musique concrète*, a leading fashion among the post-war avant-garde. But what Britten was after was a kind of documentary realism, a musical factuality to accompany the images of the train departing.

Yet, because the sound effect was musically conceived, was in fact *composed*, there was none of the customary friction between the two worlds of sound—'noise' and music—that make up the sound-tracks of most films: in *Night Mail* both worlds were imagined by the composer and subjected to the control of his ear. Hence the *totality* of the integration of sight and sound, which remains one of the film's glories and was undoubtedly its principal technical achievement. (Its only rival perhaps was *Coal Face* (1935), which was the first of the GPO films on which Britten and Auden worked together.)

On 10 January, work continued 'vigorously & solidly all day' on the music for *Night Mail*, and on the 12th, the music was finished. On the 15th ('A very cold day—again') work seriously began on recording the music for *Night Mail*. Britten's detailed entry for this day deserves virtually complete quotation. It throws a great deal of

light on the demands made of his expertise and on the kinds of
techniques he was learning and developing:

> Up early & get to Soho Square at 9.45. Some bother over parts of
> orchestra, but I eventually get down to Blackheath at 11.0 for big
> G.P.O. recording. A large orchestra for me—Fl. Ob. Bsn. Trpt.
> Harp (Maria Korchinska—very good), Vln., Vla., Vlc., CB.
> Percussion and wind machine—a splendid team. The music I wrote
> really comes off well—&, for what is wanted, creates quite a lot
> of sensation! The whole trouble, & what takes so much time is
> that over the music has to be spoken a verse—kind of patter—
> written by Auden—in strict rhythm with the music. To represent
> the train noises. There is too much to be spoken in a single breath by
> the one voice (it is essential to keep to the same voice & to have no
> breaks) so we have to record separately—me, having to conduct
> from an improvised visual metronome—flashes on the screen—a
> very difficult job! Legg speaks the stuff splendidly tho'. Recordings
> last from 11.0—12.30—lunch—3.15—5.30. So pretty dead.

What was recorded on 15 January 1936 proved to be one of the
most striking contributions Auden and Britten made to film in the
thirties; thirty-three years on, *Night Mail* still continues to have an
active life. The final and justly famous end sequence represents a
remarkable synthesis of potent visual images, a marvellous text
from Auden, and a brilliant score by Britten.

> This is the night mail crossing the border,
> Bringing the cheque and the postal order,
> Letters for the rich, letters for the poor,
> The shop at the corner and the girl next door. . . .[26]

Although the *Night Mail* recordings had been completed, there
was much still to do in the way of editing and synchronizing them.
It is clear from the diary that all along one of the problems was
the rhythmical integration of the speech and the music—'To
represent the train noises':

17 JANUARY:
I go off early to Blackheath to help cut in the sound & also join voice
& orchestra into rhythm — incidentally discovering that by mistake I

was given wrong bands to conduct from, in some cases the voice not fitting the orchestra at all — so Pat Jackson & I start a long job of patching which lasts so long that I cannot keep a dinner date with Trevor Harvey at 7.30.

By the 28th of the month, however, it seems as if work on *Night Mail* had finally been completed.

It is, as I have said, the consummate integration of sight and sound, of words and music, that must always mark out *Night Mail* for special attention; and also, especially for the time, the innovatory approach to how the sounds were assembled. We may remember from Britten's verbal overture to 1936, which I quote on p. 28, that he described his job for the GPO Film Unit as 'writing music & supervising sounds', i.e. he was not only house (or rather studio) composer but he was also responsible for the co-ordination of everything to do with the sound-tracks of the unit's films, when special sounds or sound effects were involved. Britten himself had some interesting memories of what was involved technically in securing the right sonority for a particular passage. I remember, for instance, his recalling the realization of the characteristic 'swish' of a train passing through a tunnel, or perhaps under a bridge, in *Coal Face*. This was achieved by striking a light jazz cymbal with a hard beater and then reversing the recorded sound at high speed. That characteristically ingenious idea must have been a very early example of the new technology for sound being pressed into the service of music — more than that, pressed into *making* music — and it may have been Britten's only excursion into this field. At any rate, it was certainly a pioneering act.

His work on the sound-track for *Night Mail* is typical of the way Britten would labour and labour to contrive, to devise, the particular sound for the particular context; and he could summon up these astonishingly graphic sonorities even when faced with the most improbable collection of instruments. Inevitably, the very sharply defined graphic quality of Britten's aural imagination was greatly exercised during this period when he was so busy in the film studio and the theatre, when an ability to invent sound that will create atmosphere in a tiny number of bars or immediately complement or embody a visual image or situation is an obligatory resource — though few composers have it. Of necessity, this meant the development by Britten of a quite singular descriptive gift, though one that manifested itself in terms of pure sound — it was, one might say, a gift for mimicry in sound raised to the nth degree of imagination. He had of course always had this marvellous, well-nigh photographic ear—if the paradox may be forgiven—and he continued to use it whenever he had need of it. We hear it, as fresh as ever, in Act I of his last opera, *Death in Venice*, when the sound of the engines of the ship ferrying Aschenbach back to Venice explodes into life.[27] No one who has been on deck at that moment can mistake the mechanical shudder, rattle and clatter for anything else. This is, I suggest, a manifestation, an example of the 'pictorial' that precisely fulfils, I think, what John Grierson means when, in describing the objectives of the documentary film and its charac-teristic techniques, he talked about 'the creative treatment of actuality'; and it might well serve as a very neat summing-up of one aspect of Britten's treatment of sound.

It was not only Wystan Auden who was working at the unit. Bill Coldstream, the artist, now Sir William Coldstream, was also a member of the GPO team as a young man and still has many vivid memories of the unit and its remarkable personnel. It is particularly significant I think that as a young painter he felt drawn to film and was greatly stimulated by it because, as he has told me, film in the mid-thirties in the UK seemed to creative minds to be the up-and-coming medium, a new means of expression, open to innovation and imagination, and generating the development of new tech-niques. All this was as far away as possible from stuffy academicism, from petrified forms: hence no doubt the appeal film made to the younger generation, an appeal which went strikingly across the board—because it was not only film-makers who were making films but also painters, designers, writers and composers.

I stick to my assertion that film and especially documentary film was a genuine thirties form, a singular manifestation of the period; and surely Coldstream's recollections bear out this contention.

Painter, poet and composer—all three for a time were under the unit's umbrella.[28] It seems entirely appropriate that it was in this very same month of January (on the 22nd) that Britten recorded in his diary a lunch with Auden in Soho that was devoted to discussing 'at great length the psychology of teaching art in combination—& possibility of an Academy of Combined art'. The two young men were then joined by Coldstream and went off—I daresay still talking—in Basil Wright's car to continue work at Blackheath. There is nothing special, of course, about Britten and Auden as young artists in 1936 having a serious or even solemn discussion about the psychology of teaching art, though I doubt if that is something we should have found them doing in later life. But what is fascinating is the idea of the 'combined arts', something that surely reflects the kind of combined operation in which Auden and Britten were in fact participating at this very moment. For a combination of the arts was just what the GPO Film Unit represented and what constituted its appeal to lively creative spirits. The discussion of an 'Academy of Combined art' makes particular sense when seen in this perspective, while the particular car ride of the afternoon of Wednesday, 22 January, takes on a veritable symbolic significance since the four passengers comprised a film-maker, a painter, a poet and a composer, all of them bound for—and in some way bound to—the Blackheath studio.

Somewhat later in the year, in March, Britten made a visit to the Group Theatre where, for the second time, he saw Rupert Doone's production of the Auden-Isherwood play *The Dog Beneath the Skin* in the company of Frank Bridge and his wife:

> I take them & Basil Reeve to see Auden's 'Dog' at Westminster Theatre. It is an excellent show — with glimpses of real beauty in the choruses and a lovely sense of wit & satire all through. Of course the moral (how W.H.A. loves his moral!) is more urgent than ever to-day—when the world is sick with fear of war, & yet its bloody leaders are dragging it steadily into it.

I think all of us would know precisely what Britten meant by that parenthesis—'how W.H.A. loves his moral!'—a sharp and true observation; perhaps especially true of Auden at this particular time. Ironically, though, I think the same could be said of Britten himself, a moralist if there ever was one, and nowhere more so than in his later and indeed in his very last dramatic works. It seems to me, in his case, to be a clear legacy from the thirties, when the idea of public instruction through parable-like works of art — the whole notion of an informed, educated public—was a prominent part of the thinking of the time. But for the moment I want to return to Auden the moralist, the teacher, to that undoubtedly didactic dimension of his character which spilled over into his work for films—released and no doubt encouraged by the instructional face that the GPO Film Unit presented to the world. What better expression of the prevailing ethos, than part of Auden's own 'Letter to Lord Byron' written in 1936, when the poet was in the midst of his travels in Iceland. To Byron, writes Auden, 'A poet's fan-mail will be nothing new', and he continues:

> And as for manuscripts — by every post. . .
> I can't improve on Pope's shrill indignation,
> But hope that it will please his spiteful ghost
> To learn the use in culture's propagation
> Of modern methods of communication:
> New roads, new rails, new contacts, as we know
> From documentaries by the G.P.O. [29]

The Way to the Sea, the last film I am going to consider here, was made not by the GPO Film Unit but by an independent company, Strand Films — the same unit that had earlier been responsible for *Peace of Britain*. Once again the leading spirit in the affair was Paul Rotha, who directed the film. We find references to it in Britten's diary for December 1936, when in fact Auden stayed with him for some days in London while they planned the project together— the long end commentary was Auden's work and credited as such among the film's titles. It is another film about communications,

'Up in a balloon, boys!' Hedli Anderson performing
one of her favourite music-hall songs (1930s)

Left: A publicity photograph of Britten (late 1930s)

Below: Auden, Stephen Spender and Christopher Isherwood on Rügen Island (1931)

Top L-R: Auden, William Coldstream and Britten posing as 'The Three Graces'
at the Downs School, Colwall (June 1937)

Above: Auden with Hedli Anderson and William Coldstream
at The Downs School, Colwall (June 1937)

Isherwood and Auden in Central Park, New York (1938)

another film about trains. The basic idea was a typically thirties one, a salute to technological progress in communications and the benefits it brought to people in the way of freedom of movement, access to sun and sea, and a fuller awareness of their own history. *The Way to the Sea*, which was made and released in 1937, has never received anything like the critical attention paid to *Night Mail*; and I think *Night Mail* must still be reckoned to be the more poetic and lyrical of the two films. But it is precisely the factuality and actuality of *The Way to the Sea* that mark it out as an exceptionally *authentic* documentary, if I may coin a phrase, made with the particular skills that Auden, Britten and Rotha brought to it. The score, which runs for some fifteen and a half minutes, is one of the most elaborate of Britten's film scores. It includes a number of pastiche exercises for the historical sections of the film, and parodies—a mock-military march, for example—in which we can very clearly discern the youthful composer's wit, versatility and special talent for parody: it was something he was to make a lot of, a little later, in a work like the *Variations on a Theme of Frank Bridge* for string orchestra. In its own effective way, indeed, the music tellingly deflates visual images that might otherwise seem to evoke or embody patriotic or even imperial sentiments and attitudes; images, incidentally, which themselves are presented at an angle or in a context that makes one realize, with the help of one's ears and with a certain elation still, that the good old thirties practice of satirical subversion is going on before one's eyes, an elation sharpened by the thought that the film's sponsors, Southern Railways, must have been blissfully unaware of what the end commentary was up to, was really about (for in the text too there emerge from time to time familiar thirties preoccupations, though quietly or obliquely stated). In short, irony was a weapon very deftly employed by the makers of *The Way to the Sea*,[30] in which the advance in civilization represented by the electrification of the line from London to Southampton, prompted Auden to adopt his most magisterial, instructional, moralizing, 'GPO' manner, and to utter a few—quite a few—Audenesque home truths about humankind:

The line waits,
The trains wait,
The drivers are waiting:
Waiting for Power.

On the terminus now every kind of person is converging, each with
    his own idea of freedom,
People who work,
People who read adventure stories or understand algebra,
People who would like to be rich or brilliant at tennis,
People like you and me, liable to catch cold and fond of their
    food,
Are brought all together here by a common wish:
A desire for the sea.

They gather,
They fight for the corner seat facing the engine.
Red changes to green.
They're off.

A signal box.
A power station.

We pass the areas of greatest congestion; the homes of those who
    have the least power of choice.
We approach the first trees, the lawns and the fresh paint; district of
    the bypass and the season ticket.

Power which helps us to escape is also helping those who cannot get
    away just now,
Helping them to keep respectable,
Helping them to impress the critical eye of a neighbour,
Helping them to entertain their friends,
Helping them to feed their husbands swept safely home each
    evening as the human tide recedes from London.

But we, more fortunate, pass on.
We seek the sea.

White factories stand rigid in the smokeless air.
The pylon drives through the sootless field with power to create and
    to refashion,
Power to perform on materials the most delicate and most drastic
    operations.

Looking forward out into the country, passing the wild and the
    disciplined lives,
The sun has not lost its importance:
The growth of the living is, as ever, incalculable.
But for all the new power can do to cleanse and to illuminate,
To lessen fatigue and to move deep cutters, milkers or separators,
It is already available.

Up Haslemere Bank — a trial of strength in the years of steam, but
    today of small account.
Over the hoop of the hill, and down,
Fifty, sixty, seventy miles an hour,
To the last straight run to the rolling plain of ships and the path of
    the gull,
We seek the sea.

Here is a harbour, a dockyard, equipment for the construction of
    fleets,
A scene of pilgrimage to the student of history and the curious
    stranger.
We seek an island.

All kinds of people:
The married who have begun to get on each other's nerves,
The lonely, daring to look for an amazing romance,
The consciously beautiful, certain of easy conquest,
The careworn, the unrewarded, the childlike:

They embark for the pleasant island, each with his special hope:
To build sand-castles and dream-castles,
To eat out of doors,
To hold hands in the shadow of a fort,
To exchange confidences with strangers,
To read, to relax,
Or just to be and not to think at all.

Here are all the varieties of pleasure, permission, and condolence:
For the body a favourable weather, the caress of sunlight and the
    gradual doze;
For the athletic and beautiful the fullest opportunities to be active
    and to be admired;
For the sedentary the leisure for reminiscence and reverie;
For the children the happiness of the immediate present, the
    romping hours;
For all the pleasures of the air, the waters and the places.

Do what you will:
Be extravagant,
Be lucky,
Be clairvoyant,
Be amazing.
Be a sport or an angel,
Imagine yourself as a courtier, or as a queen.
Accept your freedom.

We seek a spectacle.
We are all invited to inspect the defences of our dreams, to review
    the taciturn aggressive devices.
Let the day commemorate the successful accomplishment of our
    past,
Let it praise the skill of designers and the anonymous devotion of
    mechanics,
Let it celebrate the artless charm of the far-travelled sailor.

Let the fun be furious,
Let the intricate ferocious machinery be only amusing,
Let the nature of glory be a matter for friendly debate among all
    these people,
Both the just and the unjust,
People like you and me — wanting to live.

Night.
The spectacle fades.
The tidy lives depart with their human loves.
Only the stars, the oceans and machines remain:
The dark and the involuntary powers.[31]

Notes

1 In a letter to Paul Rotha (15 July 1970), quoted in Rotha, *Documentary Diary* (London: Secker and Warburg, 1973), p. 132, Britten recalls that Grierson approached the Royal College of Music for 'a bright young student who could write a little incidental music for a forthcoming film [*Coal Face*].' In fact, however, Britten's 1935 diary tells us that he was first approached on 27 April by Cavalcanti (via Edward Clark), and the film in question was not *Coal Face* but *The King's Stamp*.

2 'Foreword to First Edition' in Paul Rotha, *Documentary Film* (London: Faber & Faber, 3rd Edition, 1952), p. 25.

3 See *Documentary Diary*, Chapter 6, 'The GPO Film Unit (1933–37)', pp. 114–42.

4 See *Early Auden*, Chapter 6, 'Private Places', where Auden's thirties thoughts about education and educational principles are discussed.

5 Forsyth Hardy, ed., *Grierson on Documentary* (London: Faber & Faber, 1979), p. 113.

6 Quoted in *Documentary Film*, p. 43.

7 The phrase was first used by Grierson when writing in the New York *Sun* (8 February 1926) about Robert Flaherty's *Moana*. See *Grierson on Documentary*, p. 11.

8 *Documentary Film*, pp. 69–71.

9 *Around the Village Green* (1937).

10 See Chapter 8, 'The Peace Film (1936)', in *Documentary Diary*, pp. 164–70.

11 Flute, clarinet, trumpet, percussion (cymbal, side-drum, bass-drum), piano, violin I and II, viola, cello, double-bass.

12 The manuscript score of *Peace of Britain*, in the Britten-Pears Library, Aldeburgh, shows no trace of a final chorus.

13 The *Manchester Guardian* article is reproduced in Donald Mitchell and John Evans, *Benjamin Britten 1913–1976, Pictures from a Life* (London: Faber & Faber, 1978), ill. 92.

14 See *Documentary Diary*, p. 169. Rotha quotes the Secretary of

the British Board of Film Censors: 'It was suggested that certain war scenes in the film might be the property of the War Office, who would have to be consulted.' Rotha goes on to explain that the tank, in the only 'war scene' in the film, was actually an American vehicle filmed in Texas.

15 The Peace Pledge Union was of course committed wholly to a pacifist point of view, from which any possibility of force was excluded, between nations as between individuals. The League of Nations Union, though ardent to seek for and ensure peace, was not a pacifist organization like the Peace Pledge Union. It supported the League and the League's Covenant which placed on its signatories the obligation not to employ force for the settlement of a dispute until it had been submitted to the League or to agreed arbitration. If the dispute was not resolved, then it was conceded that force might be resorted to, though only after a further 'cooling-off' period. Sanctions against aggression were one of the League's supposed punitive measures.

16 Some of the unpublished works discussed in these lectures are to be published by Faber Music, London. *Russian Funeral* should be available in 1981, and four of the cabaret songs ('Tell me the truth about love'; 'Funeral Blues' ('Stop all the clocks'); 'Johnny'; and 'Calypso') were published (in one volume) in 1980. 'Calypso', incidentally, brings us a further striking example of that consistency of imagery and invention across the years that I have already mentioned in connection with 'Rats Away!' from *Our Hunting Fathers* (see p. 37). Those who are curious should compare the railway ostinato of 'Midnight on the Great Western' (from *Winter Words*, the Hardy settings of 1953) with the railway ostinato of 'Calypso' (from 1939), which they will find to be a precise model for the train noise of the Great Western Railway. No matter that Auden's text celebrated the 'Springfield Line' bound for Grand Central Station, New York. The composer, already in 1939, had his train music established — in store, as it were: a clearly defined musical idea and sonority that was to bridge a time gap of some fourteen years.

17 It seems, however, as if Auden was not particularly sympathetic to pacifism, at least not in 1941 when he wrote to Stephen Spender: 'I have absolutely no patience with Pacifism as a political movement, as if one could do all the things in one's personal life that create wars and then pretend that to refuse to fight is a sacrifice and not a luxury.' This of course was a wartime view but it does not sound as if it were of recent adoption. The letter, a remarkably interesting one, is quoted in Charles Osborne, *W. H. Auden, The Life of a Poet* (London: Eyre Methuen, 1980), pp. 206–7. Isherwood, on the other hand, discovered himself to be a pacifist in April 1939 (see Brian Finney, *Christopher Isherwood, A Critical Biography* (London: Faber & Faber, 1979), p. 173). He has remained a tireless and convinced pacifist ever since.

18 Alan Bush, who conducted the programme on 8 March 1936, was good enough to write to me as follows about the work by Brecht and Eisler that Britten in his diary identifies as 'Expedient':

> The work which, when translated into English was given the title of *The Expedient*, received its first performance in Berlin on 13 December 1930. It is described as *Die Massnahme*, Lehrstück by Brecht, music by Hanns Eisler. I conducted seven or eight performances of it in 1936–7 in and around London with a translation by my wife, Nancy, with the massed choirs of the London Labour Choral Union. The exact dates and places where these performances took place would be very difficult to unearth as, most unfortunately, the correspondence of the L.L.C.U. was in the hands of its secretary, and on his death his widow destroyed it all.

Die Massnahme, Dr Bush tells me, has been reprinted as part of the collected edition of Eisler's works. It is now generally referred to in English as *The Measures Taken*.

19 It is not known how many of the twenty-odd people on his list Brecht in fact approached with the idea of setting up an international 'Diderot Society' to circulate papers on 'theatrical science', but it is evident that at this period he believed the views of Auden, Isherwood and Doone were compatible with his own. See *Brecht on Theatre, The Development of an Aesthetic*, Translation and Notes by John Willett (London: Methuen, 1964), p. 106.

20 Shostakovich's Piano Concerto No. 1 for piano, trumpet and strings, Op. 35 (1933). Shostakovich prepared his own reduction in a version for two pianos, and it is likely that this was the version Britten was using in 1936.

21 D. Rabinovich (translated from the Russian by George Hanna), *Dmitry Shostakovich* (London: Lawrence & Wishart, 1959), p. 164. In a private communication, Alan Bush, the conductor of *Russian Funeral* at its first performance in 1936, makes an illuminating comment about the provenance of the 'funeral song': 'The tune dates from 1905, the funeral march having been written or at any rate played at the funeral which followed the massacre by the Guards of the demonstrators who assembled outside the Winter Palace on 22 January of that year.'

22 Slater's savage left-wing humour was much in evidence in *Pageant of Empire*, which was first performed by the Left Revue on Sunday, 28 February 1937. Britten's diary records the composition of the music:

20 FEBRUARY:
In morning I work at music for the Left Review [sic] — Montagu Slater's very amusing & provoking Pageant of Empire. I finish sketching three or four little Music Hall songs.

It is perhaps worth remembering that this was also the time when both the composition of the score for *F6* and the rehearsals of the play were simultaneously in progress, as the rest of the entry for 20 February makes clear:

Rehearsal [of *F6*] at Mercury all aft — very annoying, Rupert [Doone] is really beyond all endurance sometimes — his appalling vagueness & quasi-surrealist directions — & completely impractical for all his talents.

Thereafter the two projects continue in inextricable (and dissonant) counterpoint, e.g.:

21 FEBRUARY:
Work at Left Theatre stuff in morning & Montagu comes to tea in aft to hear it & discuss it. Then I spend a hectic evening copying & sketching more stuff for F.6.

23 FEBRUARY:
Finish the overture [for *F6*] & copy parts in morning & then at 2.0 I
go off to M. Theatre for a short rehearsal. Back here for tea to which
Grace Williams comes to see Beth. Then back to Theatre at 6.30 to
play percussion (Vera Dart being engaged elsewhere) for dress
rehearsal. Everything goes abominably—Rupert drives me crazy
(I'm dog-tired after Sunday & last nights) by saying in dozens of
places "We must have more music here & here & here" — regardless
of the fact that it takes time to write & rehearse music. Back here by
12.30—& find telephone message of frantic nature from Left
Theatre clamouring for more music—Oh God.

24 FEBRUARY:
Spend morning playing for a ghastly Left Theatre rehearsal — dash
(without lunch) to Mercury where I rehearse a bit & learn (to my
anguish) that they intend to cut the big final scene—including a lot
of the best music—including the Blues—my protests are unavail-
ing. Back here to work–work–work at scoring piddling bits of music-
hall stuff for Sunday. . . .

Britten finished his score for *Pageant of Empire* on 26 February, the
day of the first performance of *F6*. (Despite Britten's fears, the Blues
clearly was *not* cut: see also pp. 122–4.) On Sunday the 28th, when
the Left Revue performance took place, he was away for the weekend
at Friston with the Bridges. But we know from a letter (1 March 1937)
he wrote from Friston to Montagu Slater's wife, Enid, that he was
seeking tickets for the subsequent performance of *Pageant of
Empire*, on the following Sunday, 7 March. In the event however
Britten seems not to have gone to the performance (he had a family
supper at home) but to a rehearsal:

7 MARCH:
David Layton comes to tea & then we both go to see rehearsal of
'Blimps' Parade' section of Left Revue. It goes quite well.

In the 'Blimps' Parade' section, which Britten refers to in his diary,
a chorus of young men drills with Indian clubs. The number
included the following verse:

Christmas is coming,
   You've got to get fit.
The market's booming,
   The brandy's lit.
Chamberlain's paying
   The odd billions
For your flesh and bone
   And not your opinions.

Do you say you want food?
   You must be demented.
For feeding the fodder
   Is unprecedented.
The fodder's for feeding
   Chamberlain's guns,
And feeding the fodder
   It just isn't done.

Slater's *Stay down miner*, with incidental music by Britten, was first produced at the Left Theatre in London on 10 May 1936. Britten's manuscript of the 'Wind Song' from the play is reproduced in *Benjamin Britten 1913–1976, Pictures from a Life*, ill. 91.

23 This was probably Bridge's Piano Trio No. 2 (1929), which Irene and Bernard Richards had performed with Britten at Cambridge on 23 February 1936.

24 It is a phenomenon faithfully documented in Isherwood's novel, *The Memorial*, first published in 1932: 'One day [Eric Vernon had] come in tired and found a strange book lying in his bedroom—*Mrs Eddy*. He was in an absurd, resentful mood. He remembered a friend of his mother's, a Miss Prendergast. She lived in the village. All at once he'd seen a vile loathsome plot to do a little stealthy propaganda. He'd stalked in to confront his mother: "How did this book get into my room?"' And so on. Eric's war-widowed mother, Lily, *would* very probably have taken to Christian Science; and the passing round of Mrs Baker's *Science and Health, Key to the Scriptures* (1875) was a popular form of proselytization among 'Scientists'.

25 This was the film, issued in 1937, in which Auden appeared in the role of Father Christmas. See B. C. Bloomfield and Edward Mendelson, *W. H. Auden, A Bibliography, 1924–1969* (Charlottesville: University Press of Virginia, Second Edition, 1972), p. 257.

26 *The English Auden*, p. 290. A page from the manuscript score for this section of *Night Mail* is reproduced in *Benjamin Britten 1913–1976, Pictures from a Life*, ill. 94.

27 Benjamin Britten, *Death in Venice*, Full Score (London: Faber Music, 1980), p. 28, fig. 28.

28 Mendelson (*Early Auden*, Chapter 13, 'Parables of Action: 2') gives a remarkably full and fascinating account of Auden's relationship with the GPO Film Unit, which he left after less than six months. But although his resignation took effect during the early months of 1936, and despite his disillusionment with the GPO Film Unit, Auden was still willing to undertake another film with

Britten at the end of the year, though this time for one of the independent companies, Strand Films. This was *The Way to the Sea*, which I discuss on pp. 88–9. Ironically enough, it was directed by Paul Rotha, a review of whose seminal book, *Documentary Film*, by Auden in the *Listener* (19 February 1936) disclosed the poet's doubts about the documentary movement and earned the ire of John Grierson. (The review is included in *The English Auden*, pp. 354–6.)

29 *The English Auden*, pp. 169–99.

30 Since I wrote this, Paul Rotha has confirmed to me the ironic intention of the makers of the film.

31 Auden's end commentary has been patiently and skilfully transcribed from the sound-track of the film by Jill Burrows. I am no less grateful to Rosamund Strode, of the Britten-Pears Library, who with equal patience transcribed the text written (by Britten) into the autograph score of his music for *The Way to the Sea*. The written and spoken texts differ not inconsiderably: for example, there are sizeable gaps in the version found in the MS score, which have been filled out from the sound-track, and many minor variants. Clearly, much was amended and finally established only when words and music were actually put together in the studio. The written text has served as a useful model for punctuation and layout, and for the parts which exist only as speech, spoken rhythms and the commentator's pauses have been the editorial guide.

26 FRIDAY (57-308)

Finish soon of left theatre stuff in morn.
& code it up & copyist after lunch —
I have held them up so long with this
orchestral stuff but it has been a difficult
time. Rehearse a little with Toni Brosa
for a concert — 4°) at his studio in aft.
Back here & change for to-night's first
performance of F.6. & Mrs. Peter Burra
comes with me. It goes down very well,
& I think is pretty sure for a long run. I
feel it is a grand play — spoilt by the
omission of the end scene (but if it is
transferred to the West End that may be
remedied.) After the show we all
have a good party at the theatre &
then feeling very cheerful we all sing
(all cast & about 20 audience) my blues
two or three times as well as going thro'
most of the music of the play. Then I
play & play & play, while the whole cast
dances & sings & fools, & gets generally
wild. In fact have a good & merry
time (& me not far from being the centre of
attraction strange as it may seem!).
Bed, after coffee out, about 2.30

---

7 Britten's diary: 26 February 1937 © The Britten Estate

III.   Schoolroom and Cabaret

The schoolboy world, in the most singular way, became one of the prime sources of imagery for thirties writers — a whole new stock of symbols was introduced into literature which had its origins in the sportsfield, playground, classroom, chapel and school hall.[1] School was an often bizarre community made up, whether staff or boys, of eccentrics and misfits, and through which stalked weighty symbolic figures embodying Authority—Headmaster, Chaplain, Matron, Headboy, Prefect, and so on. In discussing *Paid on Both Sides*, Auden's charade of 1930, Samuel Hynes makes a point about the way 'the dialogue shifts back and forth between the saga-world of the blood-feud [the main substance of the drama] and what seems to be the small talk of an English public school, all about swimming matches and rugger teams'; and he goes on to quote Isherwood on this curious, at times surrealist mix:

> The saga-world is a schoolboy world, with its feuds, its practical jokes, its dark threats conveyed in puns and riddles and under-statements. . . . I once remarked to Auden that the atmosphere of *Gisli the Outlaw*[2] very much reminded me of our schooldays. He was pleased with the idea: and, soon after this, he produced his first play, *Paid on Both Sides*, in which the two worlds are so inextricably confused that it is impossible to say whether the characters are really epic heroes or only members of a school O.T.C. [Officers' Training Corps, as it was then].[3]

For reasons that are not clear to me, Professor Hynes ascribes this exploitation of school, its images, its personnel, its lingo, to *literary* sources: boys' school literature (here he seems to make too much of

Isherwood's comment) and the autobiographies of First World War poets and writers. But much of this, I feel, is superfluous explication, though I certainly think it probable that it was Kipling's use of capitals that engendered Auden's. [4] The truth is surely that Auden and his contemporaries were drawing on their own experience, and in particular on their personal experience of a particular public school, Gresham's School, Holt, which for a relatively brief but memorable period was responsible for educating some of the brightest and most unusual boys, not only Auden and Britten—though their schooldays did not coincide, Auden being much Britten's senior—but also a host of others who, in time, were to constitute a remarkable and influential intellectual élite. This may seem a curious accident of history but in fact Gresham's was a school which represented one of those pockets of change which introduced a substantial liberalism into the public school system after 1900; and it was no doubt the school's progressive reputation that was responsible for its success and particular appeal, especially to liberal and thinking parents. [5] Even so, the school's honour system, which seems to have induced crippling feelings of guilt in some boys, stimulated Auden in later life to write: 'I believe no more potent engine for turning [boys] into neurotic innocents, for perpetuating those very faults of character which it was intended to cure, was ever devised.' And in a striking sentence from the same text, which is also a peculiarly illuminating one, especially if we read it in the light of Auden's work for the theatre, he said: 'The best reason I have for opposing Fascism is that at school I lived in a Fascist state.' [6] Auden, then, did not need to look to literature for his inspiration: he looked to life.

Out of the experience of school, with all its appropriate furnishings and laws and personnel, Auden, along with other thirties writers, created a world which could effectively symbolize the repressive, tyrannical and narrow authoritarianism which stalked the corridors and infiltrated the classroom and even the dorm. It was a world, a set of values, that young radicals were determined to subvert; and the instrument of subversion, more often than not, was a corrosive satire—a by no means ineffectual means of demolition, especially of the bogus, the callous and the pompous.

We have to bear in mind, though, that this school mythology was very much a private world, an in-world, the keys to which were possessed only by those sharing the same—that is to say, pre-dominantly middle-class—background. A working-class reader could hardly have made much of the mythology of, say, Auden and Isherwood, which had its origins in an entirely different, not to say alien, educational experience. The liking for the private joke, the clannishness of the thirties, is undeniable. But despite the esoteric nature of the imagery, the intent behind the use of it was often serious and critical, questioning the validity of the values embodied in the public school tradition. It was in its way an influential protest and, in so far as it transcended the limitations imposed on it by the private mythologies of the participants, it contributed valiantly, if from a somewhat eccentric angle, to the puncturing and deflation of old deceits and, if only obliquely, to the search for new values in, and new means of organizing, education.

Britten was certainly close to these private mythological worlds, and he was vigorously engaged as a composer in many of those theatrical projects in which anti-authoritarianism was a leading theme. His brother Robert was a schoolmaster and Auden himself, when back from Spain in 1937, after a brief spell working for the Republican Government, returned to schoolmastering, this time taking up an appointment at the Downs, a prep school at Colwall, near Malvern. Because of a project that was in the air at the time, rather promisingly entitled *Up the garden path*[7] — a programme (see p. 106) of bad poetry and bad music devised for the BBC and broadcast on the Regional wavelength on 13 June—Britten found himself on a trip to Colwall, with one of the other participants in the venture, John Cheatle, to work further on the idea with Auden. There were two visits and reading Britten's diary entries takes us with an extraordinary immediacy into the very interior of that private world of the private school, which these brilliant and clever young men had, so to speak, invaded, and made their own territory. These entries surely tell us how it was — this is the stuff of the experience out of which the plays, the poems, the music, were created:

PROGRAMME AS BROADCAST
REGIONAL

SUNDAY JUNE 13TH 1937

9.56-10.31

'UP THE GARDEN PATH'

A recital of verse and music.
The verse chosen by W.H. Auden
The music by Benjamin Britten
Presented by John Cheatle.

Cast:- Charlotte Leigh   Denis Arundell
        Felix Aylmer   V.C. Clinton-Baddeley

At the piano Henry Bronkhurst, and Denis Arundell.

Music: Funeral March   Chopin
        Bump   Heinrich Frobel
        April Horn   Music by Robert Batten,
                           words by John Dowers Boosey
        Study   Bertini Album copyright 1911,
                                               Augener.
        Les Cloches du Monastere   Lefebure-Wely
        Night Hymn at Sea   Music by A. Goring Thomas
                                   words by J.Williams Mrs. Hemans
        Il Corricolo   Durand de Grau

Poems: 'Flo's letter'   Anon.
        'The Toys'   Coventry Patmore
        'King Robert'   Longfellow
        'The uninvited   Anon.
        'Blackbird'   T.E. Brown
        'The Bells'   E.A. Poe
        'The Female
              Friend'   The Rev. Cornelius Whur
        'Temple of
              Nature'   Erasmus Darwin
        'Napoleon and the
        British Soldier'   Thomas Campbell

        Selections from   Shakespeare.

8 The 'Programme as broadcast' billing for *Up the garden path*

5 JUNE 1937 [a Saturday]:
. . . catch 12.45 [train] with [John Cheatle] to Malvern. Arrive there
about 3.30 & find no connection to Colwall—so wait for bus,
which is full, so have to taxi. Meet Wystan Auden (who is teaching
in a prep school — Downs) & see about the plan & talk with him. He
has another friend staying with him — a Brian Howard, a very clever
man, intellectual but surprisingly foppish & affected. But definitely
amusing. Eat at hotel [Park Hotel] in the evening & then go to the
music rooms where we play & sing (bellow) the bad music I've found
for the 'Up the garden path' that we are here to work on. . . .

6 JUNE:
Up early & walk down to see Elms school (where Robert taught)
before breakfast. Work hard at the programme in the morning with
W.H.A. & J.C.—Doing some good stuff. Then at 12.30 I give a
small concert to some of the boys — delighting their simple hearts
with fireworks of the most superficial & Victorian manner (var. on
Home Sweet Home — Polkas and galops etc). But they are splendid
kids. We all have lunch with the school. Work again in afternoon.
Eat with school in evening & then in hotel—fool about quite
irresponsibly—Brian H. is the promoter of this. . . .

I should certainly like to have heard the improvised variations on
'Home Sweet Home'. Next day, Britten and Cheatle caught an
early train to London and life followed a different course for a few
days. But on the 15th Britten returned to Malvern, this time in the
company of Hedli Anderson, the singer—who was later to marry
Louis MacNeice—and William Coldstream, the painter, a
colleague at the GPO Film Unit, who were also bound for Colwall:

Wystan Auden meets us at Colwall & delivers us each to his (or her)
respective lodgings. Little cottages — being cheaper than the Hotel,
where however we eat tonight. Make noises in the music rooms
after.

16 JUNE:
Spend day making alterations in the cabaret songs & also in giving
concerts to the boys of the Downs school—one in lieu of a French
lesson—Wystan is a very unconventional master! The boys & staff
(mostly) are charming—& things go with an immense swing.

Play a little tennis with Bill [Coldstream]—terribly steady stuff.
Tea with Miss Woodhams—music mistress—a charming person.
  After dinner at Hotel we all go along to Mr. Fields [Maurice Field]
—the art-master—who is very intelligent & pleasant. Then we play
& sing indefinitely. We lunch with the boys. Everything is going
swimmingly—we couldn't be a better suited or happier party—
Wystan's brilliance, Hedli's intelligence & art, Bill's integrity & dry
wit—& my dullness (& youth—my only virtue) as a complete foil.

We note once again, even on this high spirited occasion, Britten's
habitual feeling of anxiety about his youth, about his inability to
keep up with his brilliant companions. But this seems to have been
only a momentary loss of self-confidence, for the next day, 17 June:

  A tremendous amount of work—rewriting things, doing a new
  version of F6. blues, which we try on the boys — & a great success it
  is too.
    The place is grand, & weather lovely & company as good as
  ever. . . .

  18 JUNE:
  Unfortunately have to pack up in the morning & deliver luggage to
  station—before spending the morning up at the school. Bill is
  staying on for 2 weeks—painting Wystan & one of the boys. Hedli &
  I catch 1.21 back to town. . . .

And so the visit to the Downs ended. The school, presumably,
returned to a more orthodox curriculum, though it is hard to
believe that the place can have been quite the same again after such
an extravagant interruption.
  We have seen in the entry for 16 June that Britten was working
on his cabaret songs while at the Downs and that at least one of
them—a version for solo voice and piano of the blues number
from *F6*, 'Stop all the clocks'—was tried out on the boys. (I shall
have something to say about the original version of the same
blues — how it was performed in the play itself — a little later.) The
songs were written for Hedli Anderson, who is mentioned in the
diary entries, possibly at her invitation: she was to specialize in the
singing of intelligent, witty, high-quality 'light' music. The idea of

a serious composer and poet writing cabaret music had its origins in Germany, and more especially in Berlin, where the pungent, sometimes abrasive cabaret song was a genre in its own right and for which memorable precedents had been provided by Brecht and Weill. Auden's and Britten's songs were personal rather than political and took as their model either the blues, roughly in the shape in which it had been imported from America, or the popular song. For instance for 'Tell me the truth about love', the model, for the text and the music, was clearly Cole Porter, and the song adopts the classical popular song shape. We have a well-defined 'intro' and a seductive refrain, seductively harmonized:

Ex. 8

And of course the topic, how to define love, was an abiding preoccupation of Auden's—we shall come across another example of it in my last lecture. No less characteristically, the song opens like a dictionary, 'Liebe—L'amour—amor—amoris':

> Some say that Love's a little boy
>   And some say he's a bird,
> Some say he makes the world go round
>   And some say that's absurd:
> But when I asked the man next door
>   Who looked as if he knew,
> His wife was very cross indeed
>   And said it wouldn't do.

Does it look like a pair of pyjamas
  Or the ham in a temperance hotel,
Does its odour remind one of llamas
  Or has it a comforting smell?
Is it prickly to touch as a hedge is
  Or soft as eiderdown fluff,
Is it sharp or quite smooth at the edges?
  O tell me the truth about love. [8]

The boys would not have had a preview of that delicious song
which did not materialize until later — the text belongs to January
1938, the month in which Auden left the UK en route for wartime
China, accompanied by Christopher Isherwood. The night before
their departure, a party was given in their honour in a London
studio, at which Hedli Anderson, with Britten at the piano,
performed some of the cabaret songs, among which, surely, must
have been the *F6 Blues*, in its solo format, a number intimately
associated with the two travellers and with some of the most
prominent of the other guests.

By all accounts, the party was a somewhat fraught and tense
gathering, stage-managed—if that is the right word, and it
probably is—by the volatile Rupert Doone: 'There were strained
relations between certain guests', as Isherwood laconically puts it in
his autobiography. One may assume, I think, that strains and
struggles of that character were absent when the *F6 Blues* was sung
to the boys at the Downs. I shall be returning to this particular
cabaret song later and perhaps can confine myself here to a
comment on the text, which Auden modified for the solo version,
supplying two new final verses, the last reading:

The stars are not wanted now; put out every one,
Pack up the moon and dismantle the sun,
Pour away the ocean and sweep up the wood;
For nothing now can ever come to any good. [9]

It is a powerful number, for reasons that I shall be spelling out, and
even now, forty years later, one has to remark on the wonderful

eccentricity of that bleak and pessimistic message being delivered to
an audience of prep schoolboys in the Cotswolds in 1936.

I have thought it worthwhile to give some space to the high jinks
at the Downs in June 1937 because they seem to me to represent
very engagingly the spirit of the times, to show, moreover, the
private mythology of the school being acted out in what were surely
highly conservative and decorous surroundings. It is impossible—
one does not even need to read much between the lines—not to
view the visits as embodying something of the surrealist spirit that
was certainly part of the mythology: 'Wystan is a very unconventional master . . . make noises in the music rooms after . . . we
play and sing (bellow) the bad music I've found for the 'Up the
garden path' . . . delighting their simple hearts with fireworks of
the most superficial and Victorian manner (var. on Home Sweet
Home—Polkas & galops etc.)' That kind of collage, built up from
successive entries, has distinctly surrealist overtones: '. . . tennis
with Bill . . . tea with Miss Woodhams . . . .' All that is lacking is
any of the sinister, threatening implications that were also part of
the private mythology's stock-in-trade. But this was a happy
mythical exercise, part nonsense and part hard work; and in
Britten's case, whose own prep school had been not only barren of
culture but positively hostile to any manifestation of it, the trip
must have been a nice way of revenging himself retrospectively on
the mean spirit of South Lodge School at Lowestoft in the twenties
by giving the 'splendid kids' of the Downs what he had never had
the chance of experiencing himself. It was also a sign to the boys,
among many other things no doubt, that music was not only fun
but required the same degree of training, discipline and expertise as
tennis, football or cricket. This was carrying the war against the
philistines into their own territory with a vengeance, with satire, we
note, as one of the main weapons in our young artists' repertoires. It
says much for the sang-froid of Miss Woodhams that the tea party
with the young composer of the glittering (but possibly vacuous)
variations on 'Home Sweet Home' seems to have been such a
success.

A contrary view of the school mythology was voiced by Cyril

Connolly, whose experience of Eton led him to propose a 'Theory of Permanent Adolescence':

> . . . the experiences undergone by boys at the great public schools, their glories and developments, are so intense as to dominate their lives, and to arrest their development. From these it results that the greater part of the ruling class remains adolescent, school-minded, self-conscious, cowardly, sentimental and in the last analysis, homosexual. [10]

But while this may hold true for some members of the thirties generation, who perhaps remained retarded in their adolescence with a fixation on school, it does not seem to say anything very interesting or enlightening about the fruitful ways that thirties artists found of turning the school experience into material for their art. One certainly cannot deny the *importance* of that experience to the generation: it seems to have been an absolutely central one, at least for the sons of middle-class families. What is particularly interesting is to see Britten as part of that process, of that trend, and yet to observe at the same time that he showed quite pronounced characteristics that significantly distinguished him from his friends and contemporaries. Indeed, we shall come to realize as we explore his relationships with the thirties that even while he helped make the period what it was, he was not wholly of it.

It is certainly true that Britten not only had access to the private mythological world of school created by his friends but was also, if mostly in a rather light-hearted way, not averse to participating in the rites and rituals of the myth should opportunity occur, as it did briefly at the Downs in 1937. But how deeply the school experience had sunk in, above all, how easy it was to continue to see the world in terms of school and its hierarchical society, which one may not have long quitted, is sharply illustrated by an entry made by Britten in his diary on 28 July 1937, in fact not so many weeks after the visit to the Downs. He describes a meeting with a distinguished, though senior, contemporary and the imagery, I think, still makes its point:

> Hair cut—& then lunch with William Walton at Sloane Square. He is charming, but I feel always the school relationship with him —

he is so obviously the head-prefect of English music, whereas I'm the promising young new boy. Soon of course he'll leave & return as a member of the staff—[Vaughan] Williams being of course the Headmaster. Elgar was never that — but a member of the Governing Board. Anyhow apart from a few slight reprimands (as to musical opinions) I am patronised in a very friendly manner. Perhaps the prefect is already regretting the lost freedom, & newly found authority!

A waspish entry, which shows that Britten in some respects at least was as restless with shows of authority, with the conventions of the establishment, as any of his close friends. But perhaps what is more revealing is that even in artistic circles, which one would have thought liberal and liberated, this hierarchical attitude, against which Britten was reacting, albeit in the form of a joke, could still prevail; and prevail, moreover, in an implied set of relationships based on the all-powerful, all-pervasive model of school.[11] This tells us a lot about at least one segment of English society and the arts in the thirties and provides further evidence of the sort of experience out of which Auden and his associates built their private mythology.

Although the diary entry quoted above shows that the youthful Britten could sting when he wanted to, iconoclasm was specifically not his forte, not part—or at least not a natural part—of his creative personality. There was, understandably enough, a powerfully iconoclastic spirit abroad in the thirties but I find little of it present in Britten's work. It is significant, I think, to take the example we have been discussing at some length, the mythology of school, that Britten in his own art took up, or rather maintained, an independent line of his own. I am sure he identified himself with the anti-authoritarian sentiment of his closest friends and their symbolic rejection of school; but it is absolutely clear that school also meant something quite different to Britten, something that did not at all exclude his clear perception, at a very early stage in his life, of the false values and orthodoxies school embodied, demanded of its members, and vigorously practised. (School was an institution that actually practised what it preached. Hence the horror of it, for so many of us.)

For Britten, school clearly meant the world of childhood, of children, of youth; and if anything, what surely roused his indignation about school, what mattered to him personally, was not so much the corrosive or downright frustrating influence of authority, as the impact of Experience on Innocence (in the Blakean sense). If the school were for a time symbolically (or indeed actually) the world for those who were its members, then Britten was certainly troubled, from his own youth onwards, by the nature of the experience that could be encountered, and profoundly disturbed by the possible destruction of the innocence that he came to believe was an essential part of the child, of the condition of childhood. Hence, undoubtedly, his love of children, his intense awareness of what they represent in terms of clear-sightedness, directness and sharpness of feeling and natural beauty, and his no less intense awareness of the perils that experience brings. It is very much, as I have already suggested, a Blakean concept of the child, though it was reached quite intuitively: Blake was not, I believe, a poet with whom Britten was in any very comprehensive way familiar at the time of which I am speaking.[12] Small wonder, though, that some years later he showed himself to be an incomparable setter of Blake's texts: the poet's and the composer's visions proved to be virtually identical.

For Britten, then, the image of school—though it may indeed have thrown off some of the resonances that it had for Auden and others—was not wholly to be rejected; it was not a totally hostile environment and was certainly not a totally negative experience. It is altogether characteristic of him that he should have made something positive out of his own experience as a child and as a schoolboy; something in fact that developed into one of the major themes of his creative life: the conflict between Innocence and Experience, with Innocence often symbolically represented by a child or youth. We witness the huge transformation of this early experience, that can nevertheless be related directly to Britten's concept of the world of childhood, and thus necessarily involving his attitudes to authority, in a whole series of major dramatic works including *The Turn of the Screw, Billy Budd* and *Owen Wingrave*. The complete list would be a long one and the permutations striking in their richness and diversity. But one important dimension of his art does not so much transform or permute as make a direct confrontation with the experience of the 'schoolboy world', a confrontation out of which emerged those works of Britten's that were written specifically for young performers, for boys and girls at school, for the institution of school. These were composed out of his perception—as clear as a child's—of what the child's world is and an exact appreciation of its potentialities in terms of musical techniques, both existing techniques and those that might have to be created specially for the realization of a particular work's sound-world. Britten's clear, childlike perception of exactly what it meant to be a child invites comparison with Walter de la Mare whose poetry was very much an enthusiasm of his as a boy and who was undoubtedly an important influence on the way in which he perceived the world of the child.

The innovating spirit that Britten brought to music for the young, to 'school music'—and I use that only as a label of convenience—had been there from the start but it made a major breakthrough in two works from the late forties, *Saint Nicolas* (1948) and *The Little Sweep* (from *Let's Make an Opera* (1949)): the children's opera attracted very wide attention and was taken up for performance by school and amateur groups all over the country (and even overseas). One would not be wrong in thinking that from one point of view this deliberately 'useful' music, with a clearly defined social and practical goal, reflects some of the educational ideals current in the thirties; it certainly owes a lot to the repertory of practical techniques Britten amassed during that decade. At the same time how distinctly *apart* from thirties ideology this music stands! There is certainly not a trace of the iconoclastic, cynical, surrealistic or pessimistic to be found in Britten's 'school' pieces; and if one can speak of hostility at all in this context, then it exists only in the sense that the pieces were indeed hostile to all the shoddy music that children had been fed, annihilating their natural good musical taste and encouraging instead an appetite for the sugary, the second-rate, the whimsical and the inane. This was a battle that Britten was fighting, educationally, with and through these works; and it was an altogether different battle from that implied by the school mythology of his thirties friends, a mythology I would suggest that did not touch him very deeply or influence him very significantly. The point is, I think, that he already had his *own* school mythology in his satchel, which he carried with him to the thirties, and indeed in part fulfilled, acting it out in his own way by writing, between 1933 and 1935, *Friday Afternoons* for his brother and 'the boys of Clive House, Prestatyn', where Robert Britten was headmaster.

Friday Afternoons is a set of twelve children's songs with piano accompaniment, which very simply but with conspicuous tech-nical skill and assurance raised the concept of the unison song to a new level. I think we may have forgotten just how malevolently bad — folksong apart — the genre of the unison song so often was in the thirties, and how depressed an activity 'class singing' could be, because of the debased standard of the materials. Britten's intense empathy with children, his capacity to invent sound which is emblematic of the imaginative world of children: those are charac-teristics with which we were to become familiar in works since the forties. But they were already manifest and vivid, even though on a modest scale, in songs like 'There was a Monkey' from *Friday Afternoons*. This is certainly not music over which one wants to pour a flood of inappropriate words which would only mask its spontaneously childlike character and melodic freshness: there is a kind of vernal innocence about it. One only marvels a little that the same imagination that brought forth the urban sophistication of 'Tell me the truth about love' could also run to this, though it is my guess that the continuously varied piano part was probably very much in the spirit of the improvised variations heard by the boys at the Downs some years later.

It is time to desert the classroom, to return to 1936 and if not precisely to cabaret, then at least to the theatre—distinctly a related area, and one with which Britten's links were growing. He had already written music for the Group Theatre,[13] for the 1935–36 season, and now, in March 1936, he was on the verge of making a memorable contribution to the development of the group. The Group Theatre had been founded in 1932 and its gifted but apparently inordinately egocentric and temperamental leading spirit was Rupert Doone.[14] We tend to think of the thirties almost exclusively in terms of brilliant personalities. In fact, the decade was extraordinarily rich in institutions and organizations, often small ones, of a particular thirties character. There were many little theatre groups (not to speak of the many small, independent film units) which generated a remarkable amount of activity and valuably introduced into the UK some very distinguished work— and challenging ideas—from Europe. The Group Theatre was not, I think, ideological in character: its only ideology, sometimes for better, sometimes for worse, was Rupert Doone himself. Ideology was the province rather of a group like Unity Theatre or the Left Theatre, to name only two examples, whose political commitment was unambiguous. But the Group Theatre was adventurous and outward looking, and its repertory was open to innovation at home and to heady influences from the Continent. Indeed an outstanding merit of the company must be recognized to be its encouragement and its discovery of new talents and more particularly of new playwrights: dramatic works by T. S. Eliot (*Sweeney Agonistes*), Auden and Isherwood, Louis MacNeice, and Stephen Spender were among those produced between 1934 and 1937.[15]

Even if one were not aware of the direct experience that Auden and Isherwood had of the German theatre, so much would be deduced, correctly, from the form their theatrical collaborations took, and the attention they paid to music. In fact, we really have to think in terms of three collaborators, not two, when considering famous thirties theatrical conceptions like *The Ascent of F6*, *Out of the Picture* (MacNeice) and *On the Frontier*; and the third man, so to speak, was Benjamin Britten, whose contribution is hardly adequately acknowledged by the description 'incidental music'— or simply 'music'—that appeared in the programmes or printed texts. It is one of the practical difficulties that music, unlike literature, has to face. Though sound may have been an essential dimension of the original conception, it is not possible, as it were, to *publish* the living sounds that were an integral part of the text. Thus a play such as *The Ascent of F6* has come to be known only by its words — the composer's voice is mute. It is certainly part of my business to indicate the importance of the contribution Britten made as the Group Theatre's 'house' composer, important of course not only for the Group Theatre but also for Britten's development as a musical dramatist. It was also at this time, and specifically during the year 1936, that Britten's working and personal relationships with Auden formed a highly significant part of his life. This was no doubt because of the variety of projects the poet and composer found themselves working on together. Also there must have been a natural desire to explore further the unique creative gifts each by now had found in the other. As a result the appearances Auden makes in Britten's 1936 diary become more and more frequent.

During the day of 12 January Britten finished work on a project in which the poet was one of his collaborators: the music for the film, *Night Mail*. The evening was also Auden-orientated, for Britten took his sister Beth to the first performance of the new Auden-Isherwood play *The Dog Beneath the Skin* which was presented by the Group Theatre at the Westminster Theatre. About the play and the production and the music, Britten had interesting things to say; and since this was a field he was soon to enter himself, they are of particular interest to us now:

> There are some first-rate things in this — Auden's choruses are some of the loveliest things I know & the best part of the show was the speaking of them by Robert Speaight. As a whole the show was marred by Rupert Doone double-crossing the 'ts' and underlining every point—leaving nothing to the imagination—Some of the sets were lovely—notably the Red Light scene. Of course it was very much cut—but even might be more so—a lot of it moves too slowly I feel. [Herbert] Murrill had done the music very competently, but adding nothing to the show, I'm afraid. It was just clever & rather dull

jazz—not as amusing perhaps as the original—a common fault with satirists.

It was certainly not the last time that Britten was to have doubts about Doone's style and methods as a producer — there were to be many difficulties and tense situations in the future, especially during the rehearsals of *F6*. One notes too how Britten had a particular awareness of dramatic tempo; and that he kept a close ear on the music. He was undeniably right in principle, if Murrill's score was indeed as flat as he found it, for in that case the model being satirized, or manipulated in a satirical spirit, remains more interesting than the attempted transformation. It was not an error into which Britten fell: is he not, the Walton of *Façade* apart, our only musical satirist of any consequence and of any quality?

A year later, in 1937, Britten was to write the incidental—perhaps *not* so incidental—music for the most celebrated of the Auden-Isherwood theatre pieces, *The Ascent of F6*; and very different though that work may be from the manner and preoccupations of Brecht and his collaborators, nonetheless it could hardly have happened at all, or taken the shape it did, had it not been for the pioneering work done in the German experimental theatre in the twenties and thirties, and more particularly by that part of the German theatre that showed a strong and radical political commitment. There had developed in Europe a significant exercise in the use of a vernacular or popular musical idiom for satirical, propagandizing purposes, and undoubtedly Britten and his collaborators had learned from this. Indeed, we know beyond any doubt that at least two works with texts by Brecht and music by Kurt Weill, *Die Dreigroschenoper* and *Aufstieg und Fall der Stadt Mahagonny*, directly influenced Auden and Isherwood when they were writing *The Dog Beneath the Skin*. We also know that the names of Auden, Isherwood and Doone—what they stood for theatrically—were known to Brecht, who recognized them as sympathizers and allies.[16] The Group Theatre, in its hey-day, was a kind of English reflection of the experimental movement in the European theatre. One may ponder a little on the transformation the style underwent, if one can speak of stylistic unity in a movement so diverse and idiosyncratic, when, as it were, Berlin moved to London. It is a subject for study in itself and has many complex aspects, but one thing I think emerges with clarity: that although the satirical principle was certainly taken over by English adherents—and it was one of the chief weapons used in the politico-theatrical war waged in Europe—it was deployed with nothing like the same savagery in the English theatre. By that I do not mean to imply that the English version did not have a fine blade—possibly indeed a *finer* blade—or did not succeed in making some penetrating thrusts; but it was English irony that replaced the ferocity of European satire. I mention this transformation, not to play off Europe against England or vice versa, or to downgrade the English format. It seems to me to be an observation that tells us something significant about the nature of English society and politics at the time, and about the personalities of those involved in theatre in the thirties 'on this island', to crib a title of Auden's. Furthermore, there is little evidence, to the best of my knowledge, of any comparable influence in Europe of that obsessional preoccupation with school, and all its attendant imagery, that we have seen to be so conspicuous a feature of so much of the most talented work done in the thirties in England. I cannot forbear in this context from quoting a remark made by Ashley Dukes in his autobiography. Dukes ran the Mercury Theatre, which hosted the original production by the Group Theatre of *F6*, and in the midst of his recollections of that event, he writes:

> Radio speakers and a listening suburban pair made a double chorus to the tragedy, so that the authors were able to indulge their satire and their expressionism at the same time. From this rather uncertain background the group of Himalayan climbers stood out as remarkable dramatic portraits of boys one had met at school and never expected to meet again. [17]

But one *did* meet them again on the stage of the Mercury Theatre, as principals in Auden's and Isherwood's plays. Schoolroom and theatre at this moment are very close together indeed; and cabaret also is there, not only as generator of the curious mix of 'comic revue, light verse, popular song and serious political commentary'[18]—Brian Finney's description of *The Dog Beneath the Skin*—but also as the determining factor in the make-up of the style of the music.

I have said already that one of the problems of assessing Britten's contribution to thirties theatre has been the inaccessibility of the music. This will remain a problem until we can get a production of, say, *F6* with all the music in place mounted; and recorded for future consultation. Of one thing though I am convinced, that the integral experience of drama and music would show us Britten's gifts as a musical dramatist already established and playing a role not only in encapsulating particular dramatic incidents or events but in the shaping of the overall structure: it is there, in that sense of structure, that we can really discern the musical dramatist of the future.

We return now to the *F6* Blues, but this time as it was originally performed at the first performance; and of course to the text of the blues from the play, which differs from the modified text Auden wrote for the solo version which was heard by the boys at the Downs. The choral version (see opp.) from the play, so colourfully and yet economically accompanied by two pianos and percussion, fully reveals, as perhaps the solo version does not to quite the same extent, Britten's mastery of a popular idiom, which he was able to transform and transcend—as Herbert Murrill was evidently not able to do in his score for *The Dog Beneath the Skin*—and thus lift the blues out of its familiar environment and make it serve as a vehicle for the release of the upsurge of feeling that breaks surface with the death of James Ransom in Act II, scene v of the play; and yet at the same time, the blues retains its associations with, as it were, the cabaret world, entertainment, life's triviality. For a few timeless and ironic rather than satiric minutes, the feelings proper to the cabaret song and the funeral dirge are experienced *simultaneously* through the unifying agency of the music; and it is the disturbing simultaneity of the experience that is primarily responsible for the powerful impact the ensemble makes. Small wonder that the blues made such an impression on the first night, and that

9 A page from Britten's MS full score of the Blues from *The Ascent of* F6
   © The Britten Estate

after the performance, at an on-stage party on 26 February 1937, Britten's diary relates:

> After the show we all have a good party at the Theatre & then feeling very cheerful we all sing (cast & about 20 audience) my blues two or three times as well as going thro' most of the music of the play! Then I play & play & play, while the whole cast dances & sings & fools, & gets generally wild.

Notes

1 Long after I had finished writing this lecture, an important investigation of the subject appeared in Bernard Bergonzi's *Reading the Thirties* (London: Macmillan, 1978), 'Men Among Boys, Boys Among Men', pp. 10–37. I warmly commend this piece of work to the reader, and indeed the whole of Professor Bergonzi's book, which is one of the best and most original studies of thirties literature I have come across.

2 *Gisli the Outlaw*, an Icelandic Saga. See *The Story of Gisli the Outlaw*, translated by George Webbe Dasent (Edinburgh: Edmonston and Douglas, 1866), from p. 23 of which I quote below. It is Gisli who speaks (or perhaps one should say 'utters'): '"He must have said this because all feel it; but let us beware that it does not turn out true, for Gest says sooth about many things; and now methinks I see a plan by which we may well guard against it." "What is that?" "We shall bind ourselves by more lasting utterances than ever. Let us four take the oath of foster-brothers."' Whereupon, the Saga tells us, Thorgrim, Gisli, Thorkel, and Vestein advance to the end of a promontory, 'breathe each a vein, and let their blood fall together on the mould . . . and all touch it; and afterwards they all fall on their knees, and were to take hands, and swear to avenge each the other as though he were his brother, and to call all the gods to witness.' The wheel might be thought to have turned full circle in 1967 when, in the second of the inaugural Eliot Memorial Lectures, given by Auden himself, he had much to say about the Icelandic Sagas. 'I was brought up on them as a child,' he wrote in his Foreword to the published text, 'and they have remained ever since among my favourite works of literature. . . .' (See *Secondary Worlds*, The T. S. Eliot Memorial Lectures for

1967 (London: Faber & Faber, 1968), 'The World of Sagas', pp. 49–84, and Foreword, p. 12.) In 1969 he published his own translation (with Paul B. Taylor) of Icelandic mythological poems, *The Elder Edda* (London: Faber & Faber).

3 *The Auden Generation*, p. 50, and Christopher Isherwood, *Exhumations* (Harmondsworth: Penguin Books, 1969), p. 31.

4 For example, consider the capitals in this extract from one of Kipling's short stories, 'The Vortex', from *A Diversity of Creatures* (London: Macmillan, 1917): '"We," Penfentenyou replied ambassadorially, "have come to have a Voice in Your Councils. By the way, the Voice is coming down on the evening train with my Agent-General. I thought you wouldn't mind if I invited 'em. You know We're going to share Your burdens henceforward. You'd better get into training." "Certainly," I replied. "What's the Voice like?" "He's in earnest," said Penfentenyou. "He's got It, and he's got It bad. He'll give It to you," he said.' And so on. Of course the intention here is partly ironic and parodistic. But it is easy to see how, with a step further forward, these enormous Abstractions can take on a life, and even a threatening life, of their own. This was sometimes the case elsewhere in Kipling. But my sample suffices, I think, to make the point.

5 See Jonathan Gathorne-Hardy, *The Public School Phenomenon* (London: Penguin Books, 1979), pp. 332–54, and especially pp. 345–50.

6 *The English Auden*, p. 325.

7 See W. H. Auden, *A Bibliography, 1924–1969*. Something of the intended character of the programme can be deduced from a report that appeared in the *Daily Telegraph* (10 June 1937) in advance of the broadcast (I am grateful to Professor Mendelson, who drew my attention to it and supplied the detailed programme (see p. 106)):

Radio Topics, by a radio correspondent
'The World's Worst'
W. H. Auden, satirical poet and part author of 'Ascent of F6', and Benjamin Britten, 23-year-old composer of music, are

preparing for June 13 'Up the Garden Path', an elaborate and light-hearted leg-pull. They will gather a large and impressive list of poets and composers and then proceed to demonstrate what has often been termed the drivel that has on occasions been produced by these masters.

The programme is, in effect, a miscellany of the world's worst words and music.

Britten's diaries fill out the picture:

9 JUNE 1937
In afternoon I go to Denis Arundell's flat for a run thro' of the music of 'Up the garden path' — with [John] Cheatle, Charlotte Leigh & Clinton-Baddeley. Then to BBC. for further run thro'. It goes quite well — but rather hindered by uncontrollable laughter.

10 JUNE
Spend a long time in morning running round second-hand music shops looking for an item for the Sunday programme. Then for a time to BBC.

11 JUNE
Rehearsal of music for 'Up the Garden Path' at 10.0 at BBC. Some difficulty as some of the singers won't see that some of the music (Victorian solemn & pompous 'Night Hymns at Sea') arn't bad [sic] — so facile in expression & so clichéd. But the light stuff (in its way so good) goes so well.

13 JUNE
Return to London — which I have to do by 6.36. Straight to BBC. Eat with John Cheatle & then back there for broadcast of 'Up the Garden Path'—which goes splendidly & is really very very funny. Auden's & my collaboration with a very excellent production by Cheatle is quite successful.

8 *The English Auden*, p. 230. Britten's settings of 'Tell me the truth about love'; 'Funeral Blues' ('Stop all the clocks'); 'Johnny'; and 'Calypso' are published as *Four Cabaret Songs* (London: Faber Music, 1980).

9 *The English Auden*, p. 163. If the F6 Blues was heard at the

ill-fated party on 18 January 1938, then the final verse may have struck the right doomed note. What was clearly a less than wholly convivial gathering has been documented by Isherwood, in *Christopher and His Kind* (New York: Farrar, Straus and Giroux, 1976), pp. 293–4, and by P. N. Furbank, in the second volume of his biography of E. M. Forster (London: Secker and Warburg, 1978), pp. 222–3. See also Eric Walter White, *Benjamin Britten: His Life and Operas* (London: Faber & Faber, 1970), p. 26, whose Chapter II, 'Collaboration with W. H. Auden', was a valuable early attempt to document the relationship, and W. H. Auden, *The Life of a Poet*, pp. 148–9. To these various accounts can now be added Britten's own. His diary entry for 18 January 1938 perhaps does something to explain why the party may have got off on the wrong foot:

> I go to Isherwood where I'm staying. Change. Dinner with Stephen Spender etc. (John Lehmann & Humphrey S. [Spender] there)—colossal row—on phone Christopher & me v. Rupert Doone—eventually go on to Party given in honour for Wystan & Christopher at Trevelyan's [Julian Trevelyan, the painter] in Hammersmith. Beastly crowd & unpleasant people. Christopher leaves in temper & I spend night with J. [John Pudney] in Hammersmith.

It must have been a depressing occasion indeed for Britten to omit any reference to what everyone else remembered — the performance of his cabaret songs. Next day, 19 January:

> Early to Isherwood—& I go to Victoria [Station] to see him & Wystan off to China.

In the afternoon, a compensating experience:

> Hedli sings Wystan's & my Cabaret songs to Ralph Hawkes with great success. Catch 7.42 back to Peasenhall [Suffolk].

If only Britten had been more specific about *what* cabaret songs! There is not a title to help us out. One wonders in particular about 'Tell me the truth about love'. Professor Mendelson informs me that the probability was that Auden wrote the poem *after* his departure from the UK for China—in fact, on board ship. This would mean that the text was written very soon after the ghastly party had taken place, in which case this song could certainly not have been among those that were performed. I wonder, however, if it might not have been the case that the poem and the music were in fact very hastily done *for* the party—the idea somehow strikes the right note—and what Auden did shortly after the event was perhaps to revise and fair copy his text, which might explain his specific documentation of it?

10 Cyril Connolly, *Enemies of Promise* (London: Penguin Books, 1979), p. 271.

11 See *Early Auden*, Chapter 6, 'Private Places': 'Before this time . . . from *Paid on Both Sides* to *The Orators*, the schoolboy was the measure of all things. The adult world appeared as a public school writ large, where the fun turned ugly. Since schools educated no one to move beyond them, the adult world retained the tribal rites and immature relations of the dormitories.'

12 However, W. H. Auden, in his unpublished fiftieth birthday tribute to Britten (see also Lecture IV, n. 24, p. 169) remembers Britten setting a poem by Blake as part of a projected film score 'about Africa'. (The poem was the fourth verse of 'The Little Black Boy' from *Songs of Innocence*.) The film, as Auden and Britten conceived it in 1935, was abandoned but finally emerged in 1938 as *God's Chillun*. It was originally to be entitled *Negroes*. Part of the text appears in *The English Auden*, pp. 292–3. See also Rachel Low, *Documentary and Educational Films of the 1930s* (London: George Allen & Unwin, 1979), p. 148.

13 First, incidental music for a production of *Timon of Athens* (which included a dance for Rupert Doone) and then a score for Louis MacNeice's translation of *The Agamemnon*.

14 A characteristic reaction of Britten to Doone's temperament is found in his diary entry for 7 March 1937:

> Miss Macdonald comes to dinner—& I go with her to see F6 after —which is going splendidly—tho' the end is definitely unsatisfactory. Rupert is there—& is a confounded nuisance with his

grumbles about vague & abstract matters—like a spoilt child that
feels neglected & wants to make a fuss about something.

15 There is an illuminating account of Auden's work (and
Isherwood's) with and for the Group Theatre in *Early Auden*,
Chapter 12, 'Parables of Action: 1'. A history of the Group Theatre
is being written by Michael J. Sidnell. See also 'Documents and
Texts from the Workers' Theatre Movement (1928–1936)' by
Raphael Samuel and Tom Thomas, *History Workshop Journal*,
No. 4, Oxford, Autumn 1977, pp. 102–42. It is an odd fact that the
formation of the Group Theatre in February 1932 was almost
immediately preceded by the formation of a somewhat like-minded
Group Theatre (identical title!) in the United States, of which
the founders were Lee Strasberg, Harold Clurman and Cheryl
Crawford. Doone's group however knew nothing at the time of the
American venture, which was also to develop a musical association
with Kurt Weill. One may think it singular that the work on which
Auden and Britten were to collaborate in the States, the operetta
Paul Bunyan, was very much in the musico-theatrical tradition
created by the Group Theatre of America, of which the Columbia
Theater Associates (who gave the first performance of *Bunyan* in
1941) might be thought to have been one of many related offspring.
16 See also Lecture II, p. 71 and n. 19, p. 96.
17 Ashley Dukes, *The Scene is Changed* (London: Macmillan,
1942), pp. 201–15, and particularly p. 210. Dukes's mention of
'Radio speakers and a listening suburban pair' reminds us of the
important role allotted to radio (and its accessories and auxiliaries)
in thirties dramas. For example, MacNeice's *Out of the Picture*
opens with a Radio Set emitting the news and closes with a Radio
Announcer delivering the moral of the play in the shape of a lyric;
and in *F6* the radio is virtually one of the principal dramatis
personae. The attention paid to radio by dramatists shows how the
new medium of information had become part of the thirties
imagination.
18 Brian Finney, *Christopher Isherwood, A Critical Biography*
(London: Faber & Faber, 1979), p. 159. Music-hall should surely

also have been added to Mr Finney's inventory, a genre in which
T. S. Eliot had taken an influential interest: see his famous essay on
Marie Lloyd in *Selected Prose of T. S. Eliot*, Frank Kermode, ed.,
(London: Faber & Faber, 1975), pp. 172–4.

8 FRIDAY (8-357)

Hurriedly do some now parts (Suzonietta, this time for further reproduction) before meeting Wystan Auden at 78 Tottenham Ct. Road. He goes off to Spain (to drive a ambulance) to-morrow. This terribly sad & I feel ghastly about it, tho' I feel it is perhaps the logical thing for him to do — being such a direct person. Anyhow it's phenomenally brave. Spend a glorious morning with him (& Dupres lunar brown, coffee - drinking). Talk on everything, & he gives me two grand poems — a lullaby, & a big, simple, folk, farewell. that is overwhelyingly tragic & moving. I'm lots to do with them. Rest — feeling very sore — Peter Floud, late of Gresham's, a great friend of mine then — at Cyps Royal, & he is my niece, but naturally its hard to appreciate anyone feeling like this. At 3.42 meet them & Aunt Silvia from Friston (In. goods douni to Bromley) — bring them for bad here after tea — & then bad to meet Francis Barton in (my paramour at South Lodge) at Charing X at 7.0. Then eat & show with him. He is still a grand person — utterly different from anyone I ever meet & quite refreshing in many ways. Back Bath, Beny, Kathleen & see them for a stranger again at Pavillion.

IV.   On this Island

The month of December 1936 represented something of a peak in the association between Auden and Britten. On the first day of the month, Britten wrote in his diary:

> Wystan Auden arrives at tea-time to stay for a time while we work on the Strand Film [*The Way to the Sea*]. It will be nice having him, if I can conquer this appalling inferiority complex that I always have when with vital brains like his. After dinner he tells me he's decided to go to Spain after Xmas and fight — I try to dissuade him, because what the Spanish Gov. might gain by his joining is nothing compared with the world's gain by his continuing to write; but no one can make W.H.A. alter his mind.

A fascinating entry on two counts: on the one hand, it shows the intricate mix of personal lives and politics, so characteristic of the thirties, and also the stand that Britten felt obliged to take against Auden's decision to fight in Spain. In fact, although Auden did go to Spain, it was not to fight. But clearly in December 1936 he thought he might; and this aroused the opposition of his fervently pacifist composer friend. There is something wholly typical about Britten's implied belief that the artist's duty was to go on creating; not to participate in destruction, but instead to attempt to influence and persuade and modify. It was, I think, a point of view Britten stuck to all his life. I am sure it was this belief that led in 1961 to the composition of the *War Requiem*, to name perhaps the most famous of Britten's works in the category of what one might call public persuasion. Ironically, a disillusioned Auden came eventually to quite the opposite point of view, and he made a now well-known statement on that very point in 1939, though it was not published at the time:

Artists and politicians would get along better in a time of crisis like the present, if the latter would only realise that the political history of the world would have been the same if not a poem had been written, not a picture painted nor a bar of music composed.[1]

Britten's diary entry for 1 December, then, provokes thoughts about differences and dissonances. In fact the first, personal part of the entry, as distinct from the political part, while showing Britten's whole-hearted recognition of Auden's intelligence and intellect, also reveals what it was that eventually drove — and kept — the two men apart. As this entry among a number of others makes clear, there was a powerful feeling of intellectual inferiority on Britten's side. We must remember that he was the youngest member of the group—he was twenty-three in November 1936, while Auden was twenty-nine, Isherwood thirty-two and Doone thirty-three—and also *felt* himself to be the youngest. Furthermore, he was the supposedly 'inarticulate' musician—and I think that is how he saw himself—handy with notes but uncomfortable amid torrents of words and ideas, especially abstract ideas. This image of himself was not, in my opinion, rooted at all in reality, but fantasies influence our conduct as much as (or more than) truths; and a deep suspiciousness of what one might generally describe as intellectual theorizing remained with Britten all his life. The ostentatious, donnish exuberance that often accompanies a particular kind of verbal dexterity and mental adroitness succeeded only in discomfiting Britten. I think he had a genuine dread of being swamped by a flood of unleashed intellectual activity with perhaps no very great depth to it.

However, this was not the case with Auden. I think the problem arose, as far as Britten was concerned, out of the nature of the contrast between Auden's personality and Britten's. The poet's fearsome brilliance of mind, prodigious learning and intellectual curiosity were embodied in a person whom Britten, as the years advanced, found increasingly and dauntingly dogmatic and authoritarian in his views and attitudes; and the composer's negative reaction was of course exacerbated—exaggerated—by his own sense of 'inferiority'. Obviously other friends of Auden managed perfectly well and were not overwhelmed by the intellectual fireworks, perhaps because they realized that not all Auden's ideas were to be taken with equal seriousness, and were perhaps not taken equally seriously by Auden himself. But with Britten it was a little different, I think. Possibly his nervousness in the presence of hyper-articulateness made it difficult for him to distinguish between the brilliant but profound insight and the clever but superficial comment; and he certainly had a distinct antipathy to what he took to be intellectual 'bossiness'—'bossy' was a sharply critical term in Britten's vocabulary. I think even the warmest of Auden's admirers would agree that from time to time that 'bossiness' could be uppermost. To some it was endearing, even endearingly dotty, but to others, like Britten, it could appear impossibly authoritarian and overbearing. [2]

This was undoubtedly complicated by the very nature of Auden's verse, in which the elements of sheer verbal dexterity and verbal complexity were so prominent. There was, for a start, his mammoth vocabulary, though clearly the vigour, the inventiveness, the vividness and the marvellous strangeness of Auden's language made an enormous appeal to the youthful Britten; we shall see what a stimulus to his imagination Auden's 1936 collection of poems *Look, Stranger!*[3] was to be. On the other hand, Britten must have found the complexity, which sometimes slid into obscurity, less appealing. In my first lecture I suggested that the somewhat baffling texts of the framing Prologue and Epilogue in *Our Hunting Fathers* were the last to be tackled by the composer because their very complexity presented him with a particular musical problem. It is true that a deliberate obscurity, the reluctant public unfolding of the artist's private world of myth, was one of the techniques, one of the styles, that we associate with the thirties; and clearly Britten was willing to go along with that element of verbal obscurity which might be attributed to the times, especially when the source of it was an admired figure like Auden. But it was a willingness that was limited, and I think that once he was set tasks of immeasurable verbal difficulty to solve, challenges which he found positively *anti*-musical, the seeds of later rebellion were sown. It seems to me that already, in December 1936, at the time of a very close personal and professional relationship between Auden and Britten, we can begin to discern the cause of the friction that led finally to their going their independent ways.

I can offer an example, by looking ahead a little, of that mammoth vocabulary of Auden's that I believe Britten came eventually to find intolerably burdensome. Auden, we all know, was fascinated by words, by lexicography. Words seeped and leaked from him much as notes tumbled out of Britten. More than that, Auden could write words about words and make a very striking poem in the process, in the same way perhaps that Stravinsky could write music *about* music. My light-hearted, but I think illuminating, example comes from *Paul Bunyan*, the operetta on which Auden and Britten began work a year or so after Britten's arrival in New York in 1939. This collaboration was influenced directly by the concept of the American musical, and so it was often 'lyrics' that Auden had to supply, often with conspicuous success. One of Auden's preoccupations was the difficulty of defining the nature of love—'Tell me the truth about love', one of the cabaret songs I discussed in the last lecture, is a typical example—and it is spelled out once again in 'Love Song', from his libretto for *Paul Bunyan*:

JOHNNY: You must sing her a love song.
CHORUS: That's too hard and takes too long.
JOHNNY: Nonsense. It's quite easy, and the longer it is, the more
          she'll like it. Use the longest words you can think of.
          Like this:
                    Love Song
JOHNNY: In this emergency
          Of so much urgency,
              What can I do
          Except wax lyrical?
          Don't look satirical;
          I have empirical
              Proof I love you.

Speaking with deference,
I have a preference
   For a nice view:
Your look of spaciousness,
Your manner's graciousness,
Your limbs' vivaciousness,
Your mind's herbaceousness
Your whole palatiousness
   Makes me love you.

Some force mysteriously
But most imperiously
   Warms my heart through:
I on detecting it,
After inspecting it
Find that correcting it
Will mean reflecting it
Back and convecting it,
In fact connecting it
   Firmly with you.

My dreams compulsively,
Almost convulsively
   Show it is true:
No animosity,
Only precosity:
Eyes' luminosity
Ears' curiosity
Nose's monstrosity
Cheeks' adiposity
And Lips' verbosity
All with velocity
   Bear down on you.[4]

A wholly characteristic example of Auden's passion for word-play:
it may be a love song, but it is a song more about his love of words

than anything else. How typical that when he comes to 'wax lyrical', what he immediately turns to is the dictionary. Moreover, once the game starts, Auden finds it impossible to stop. The verses I quote above are by no means all of the song; and in the exchange between Johnny and the Chorus that follows 'Love Song', one may feel that Auden has lost not only his heart to words, but his head as well:

JOHNNY [*spoken*]:	Got the idea? Right. Now this time you join in. When I think of a word, you think of another word to rhyme with it.
JOHNNY [*sings*]:	All nouns are dedicate
	To this one predicate
	Adjective too:
	Appendectomy
CHORUS [*sings*]:	's a pain in the neck to me
JOHNNY:	Anthropomorphosis
CHORUS:	Owns several offices
JOHNNY:	Psychokinesia
CHORUS:	Never gets easier
JOHNNY:	Papal Encyclicals
CHORUS:	Are full of pricklicles
JOHNNY:	Plenipotentiaries
CHORUS:	Endure for centuries
JOHNNY:	Supralapsarians
CHORUS:	Aren't vegetarians
JOHNNY:	Hendecasyllable
CHORUS:	Makes me feel illable
JOHNNY:	Icthyosauruses
CHORUS:	Won't sing in choruses
JOHNNY:	Septuagesima
CHORUS:	Ate less and lessima
JOHNNY:	Occi-parietal
CHORUS:	O DO BE QUIET
JOHNNY:	all
	Mean:
CHORUS:	I LOVE YOU

Very amusing to read but perhaps less amusing if you're a composer faced with setting those particular words and rhythms to music. Indeed, I think it is self-evident that those texts were wholly impractical for music, using as they do a tongue-twisting vocabulary that stubbornly resists musicalization; and it was not a question of one or two intractabilities but a positive flood of them. In fact, in 1940–41 Britten dutifully got down to work and did his best, no doubt keeping his thoughts about the excessive compositional difficulties involved to himself. That he loyally got on with the job tells us something about his relationship to his poet friend at that time. Auden's powerful persona and Britten's affection and admiration for the poet meant that the composer's difficulties were swallowed or suppressed, a situation that was not to be repeated in future years. But the musical results of the exercise were not acceptable in Britten's view; and when he came to look at *Paul Bunyan* in his last years, in order to prepare it for revival in 1976, 'Love Song' and its appendix were axed. It was clear that the composer was glad to be able to get rid of the song and that his instinctive doubt about the number thirty years earlier was identical with his judgement of it in the last years of his life. [5]

I am not sure that Auden ever wholly comprehended that while words are words, words written for transformation into and by music—for consumption by music—are something entirely different. [6] I think that it was in fact an increasing inability to see this that finally brought about the end of his creative association with Britten; and there was also the equally important factor of Britten's increasing need to escape, to free himself, from an exhilarating, inspiring but ultimately dominating collaborator. The partnership worked wonderfully well, I think, while the youthful Britten himself was still developing as an artist and still had things to learn, to take, from Auden. We should not underestimate the vistas that the poet opened up for the composer in so many areas of thinking and feeling. But as soon as that need was no longer there, as soon as Britten's own creative personality had more fully emerged, and with it, a much greater sense of self-confidence and independence, the friction that had been suppressed up to this point began to make itself felt. There was not, as far as I know, an explosion which ruptured a long-standing friendship, but more of a withdrawal on Britten's part, aided of course by his return to the UK in March 1942, while Auden remained in the States. The break marked the end of one way of life and the beginning of a new; and above all it marked the burgeoning of the remarkable musical partnership with the singer Peter Pears.

It is probable that Auden was not pleased by what he considered to be a misjudgement on the part of Britten and Pears, a fracture in the solidarity of the group of quasi-exiles based on New York and Long Island in the early forties, the history of which alone forms an important part of Britten's life, and of Auden's. But while Auden wrote to a friend in 1939, 'I never wish to see England again', Britten was perpetually homesick in the States and hated New York as much as Auden loved it.

However, in 1936, the relationship was flourishing and notable collaborative enterprises were in full swing, although of course both men were also involved in independent projects. *The Ascent of F6* was on the stocks; Paul Rotha's film *The Way to the Sea*— which I discussed in my second lecture—was in the making; and the publication of Auden's second volume of poems *Look, Stranger!* meant that Britten's mind was turning already to the possibility of a first collection of settings.

One of the first fruits of Britten's assimilation of Auden's new book of poems was the setting, for two voices and piano, of a lyric the poet had dedicated to him — 'Underneath the abject willow'.[7] Auden was present at its first performance, at the Wigmore Hall on 15 December 1936. This was a time of particularly close association between the two and Britten was now beginning to feel a shade less in awe of Auden. I have already mentioned Britten's sense of intellectual inferiority but, on 4 December, a few days after Auden's arrival to stay with Britten in his flat where they were to work together on *The Way to the Sea*, Britten rather revealingly writes '. . . it's good having Wystan here & I'm losing my nervousness with him a bit'. The time was approaching, though, when the cause of Britten's sense of inferiority was temporarily to be removed. On 8 January 1937, Britten had a last meeting with Auden who was to leave for Spain the next day, or so the two friends thought. In fact, Auden's departure was delayed, as Britten records on the 10th:

> Wystan hasn't gone yet—expects to go tomorrow—because the Medical Unit he was going with was stopped by the government. Fine non-intervention that, which even stops medical aid as well as arms, to the legal government.

I think the vivid entry of the 8th, written with Auden's imminent departure in mind, is worth quoting in full:

> Hurriedly do some more parts (Sinfonietta, this time for further reproduction) before meeting Wystan Auden at Tottenham Ct. Road. He goes off to Spain (to drive an ambulance) tomorrow. It is terribly sad & I feel ghastly about it, tho' I feel it is perhaps the logical thing for him to do—being such a direct person. Anyhow it's phenomenally brave. Spend a glorious morning with him (at Lyons Corner House, coffee-drinking). Talk over everything, & he gives me two grand poems — a lullaby, & a big, simple, folky Farewell — that is overwhelmingly tragic and moving. I've Lots to do with them.

The 'big, simple, folky Farewell' to which Britten refers was Auden's long poem 'It's farewell to the drawing-room's civilised cry,/The professor's sensible whereto and why'. Auden wrote it out on the flyleaf of one of Britten's scores, the published score of the *Sinfonietta*, Op. 1, which Britten happened to be carrying with him that day as there was a performance of the work in the offing.[8] It is strange to think of this remarkable envoi to the world Auden was temporarily quitting being transcribed amid the coffee-cups in a Lyons Corner House on Friday, 8 January 1937. The farewell included a reference that was clearly addressed to the composer, for among the things that are to be put away for the duration, along with 'the brilliant stories / Of reasonable giants and remarkable fairies,/ The pictures, the ointments, the frangible wares / And the branches of olive . . .' were 'the works for two pianos'.

This particular poem was to surface again in the Spring of 1939.

In April, a festival of 'Music for the People' was mounted at the Queen's Hall, London; and Britten composed a work for it entitled *Ballad of Heroes*, for tenor solo, chorus and orchestra, with texts by Randall Swingler,[9] sometime literary editor of the *Daily Worker* and a prominent member of left-wing literary circles in the thirties, and Auden himself. The work was written to honour the men of the British Battalion of the International Brigade who had fallen in Spain, and it was conducted by Constant Lambert. *Ballad of Heroes* remains one of the most neglected of Britten's works, even though he thought well enough of it to give it an opus number, Op. 14; to have it among his published works, and to revive it at the Aldeburgh Festival of 1973. Clearly he did not see it as just a topical piece. It is not my business here to try to place *Ballad of Heroes* in the context of Britten's *oeuvre* though perhaps I can make one general musical observation about this early piece to indicate why it ought to claim the attention of students of his work as a whole: in *Ballad of Heroes*, one of the composer's many anti-militarist pieces, certain techniques are developed which foreshadow those used in the *War Requiem* in 1961. It is another case of that consistency of imagery I have already mentioned: in *Our Hunting Fathers* we encountered the identification of the tuba with pestilence; and there are many pages in the 1939 *Ballad* where particular images of war give rise to musical ideas, forms and textures that lead one to realize that the *War Requiem* was the fulfilment of firm convictions and musical preoccupations that had been established in the thirties.[10] *Ballad of Heroes* and *War Requiem*, separated though they may be by more than twenty years, belong to the same line of evolution in Britten's art, a line in which specific beliefs and specific musical techniques emerge in inextricable association.

In the central Scherzo of the *Ballad* Britten uses some of the verses of the 'farewell' poem Auden wrote out for him on 8 January 1937. By April 1939, when *Ballad of Heroes* had its first perform-ance, it was over two years since Auden had returned from Spain. He had in fact already left for the United States, accompanied by Christopher Isherwood, on 19 January 1939, by which time, as Edward Mendelson remarks, the poet 'had . . . begun to find intolerable his public role as court poet to the Left'.[11]

Part of Britten's musical activities in the thirties might be similarly categorized; and it might be said that it was still in *his* role of court composer to the Left that he wrote *Ballad of Heroes* early in 1939. By then, he was himself on the verge of leaving for the United States, which he did a month or so later, in the company of Peter Pears. So there is a fascinating and complex superimposition of farewells to be disentangled in the Scherzo of *Ballad of Heroes*: Auden's farewell on leaving for Spain in 1937, which was also a goodbye to his composer friend, and Britten's farewell to country, home and friends on his exit to North America in 1939, amid the gathering darkness in Europe:

> The fishes are silent deep in the sea,
> The skies are lit up like a Christmas tree,
> The star in the West shoots its warning cry:
> 'Mankind is alive, but Mankind must die.'

> So good-bye to the house with its wallpaper red,
> Good-bye to the sheets on the warm double bed,
> Good-bye to the beautiful birds on the wall,
> Its good-bye, dear heart, good-bye to you all.[12]

The use of those verses must have had a quite peculiar significance for Britten, must they not? One might interpret *Ballad of Heroes*, and this movement in particular, as Britten's farewell to more than his native land. *Ballad of Heroes* was the last politically engaged work of its kind he was to write, and in the Scherzo, it included his last 'Dance of Death'—a concept, as I pointed out in my first lecture, that had its origins in Auden's *The Dance of Death*, produced by the Group Theatre in 1934. There was in fact one further 'Dance of Death' to come, though it was not thus entitled—again a central scherzo, the 'Dies irae' from the *Sinfonia da Requiem*. However, by 1940, when that work was composed, the 'Dance of Death' idea had been transformed and now belonged to the area of private experience, rather than public comment. The concept disappeared along with the decade. *Ballad of Heroes* was Britten's final exercise in quasi-political commitment, and he was never to return to the style or substance of those works that helped to shape the thirties. It was, indeed, 'good-bye to you all': not only to family and friends, but also goodbye to the decade itself:

Ex. 9

As 1936 came to an end and 1937 began, Britten was not yet thinking of quitting the UK and following Auden to the States, but was fulfilling commissions, in some of which Auden was his major collaborator. In one of these, *The Ascent of F6*, Auden was an absent collaborator, away in Spain while Britten completed his music, written mainly in February 1937, although it was still occupying him when the play went into production by the Group Theatre. (See also Lecture II, n. 22, pp. 97–100.)

It must have been a relief to have Auden safely back on 5 March, especially after the ill tidings from Spain of the death of Ralph Fox.[13] The news had reached Britten just as Auden was himself about to leave:

> 6 JANUARY:
> Ralph Fox is the latest victim to Fascism in Spain — shot in action. He was a very good writer & a great loss.

With Auden back, it was as if some spring in Britten were again released; and within a couple of months his diaries are full of references to settings of Auden, the cabaret songs for Hedli Anderson among them, and more important, settings of poems from Auden's 1936 volume, *Look, Stranger!*[14] On 5 May, he begins work on the songs he finally gathered together under the title *On this Island*, Op. 11, though in fact the first song to be completed was a setting of a particularly fine lyric from *The Dog Beneath the Skin*, 'Nocturne'.[15]

> 5 MAY:
> A successful day with the 'muse'. In the morning I set a serious poem of Wystan's (from Dog-Skin)—Nocturne, & in the afternoon a light one for Hedli Anderson—Johnny.[16]

Britten worked regularly at his Auden settings over a period of some six months, completing the set of five — and it is clear that he contemplated gathering together further settings[17] by describing *On this Island* as 'Vol. I', when it was published—in October 1938.[18] The first performance of the songs, given by Sophie Wyss,

for whom Britten had written *Our Hunting Fathers*, took place on
19 November 1937:

> Rehearse at BBC. in aft. At the Contemporary Concert at 9.00 odd I
> play the piano part of my 'On this Island' songs (Vol. I)—with
> Sophie Wyss who sings them excellently—tho' her English is
> obscure at times.
>
> They have a public success, but not a succès d'estime — they are
> far too obvious & amenable for Contemporary music.
>
> Wystan comes & we — with the Gydes [Sophie Wyss's family],
> W. Walton & Lennox Berkeley, have a party after. Wystan comes
> back to the Gydes after—but as the car misbehaves, we don't get
> back till past 3.00.

But in fact there had been an earlier though private première given
by another singer, Peter Pears, with whom Britten was, in this year,
to embark on his long personal and musical partnership. On Friday
15 October Britten writes:

> Busy packing & things—after dinner Lennox B & Christopher
> Isherwood come to coffee to hear Peter sing my new songs & are
> considerably pleased—as I admit I am. Peter sings them well—if he
> studies he will be a very good singer. He's certainly one of the nicest
> people I know, but frightfully reticent.

It is not my intention here to try to present a complete account of
the songs that make up *On this Island*, nor to document in detail
their chronology. I want rather to point to their general significance
in the development of Britten's art, and to the particular significance they have as an example of his creative relationship with
Auden. With one aspect of the set we are already familiar, the
'cabaret' style; and in the very last song, 'As it is, plenty', we have
one of Britten's wittiest, sharpest and most elegant songs in this
mode, the only cabaret-like song to be published during his lifetime. The first verse of the poem sets the mordant tone:

> As it is, plenty;
> As it's admitted
> The children happy

And the car, the car
That goes so far
And the wife devoted:
To this as it is,
To the work and the banks
Let his thinning hair
And his hauteur
Give thanks, give thanks.[19]

Ex. 10

This acid number was composed a little later in the year than the cabaret songs I mentioned in my third lecture. Clearly it belongs to the same genre; but the manipulation of the style is different and new. A popular song idiom is skilfully evoked and used in order to damn the false values the poet recites, while itself escaping triviality. Without Auden's ironic, sceptical intelligence, and without all those collaborative exercises in social satire which were so conspicuous a feature of his and Britten's work in the theatre at this time, the song could scarcely have existed.

'As it is, plenty' is the most topical of the set, a poem probably written in April 1936 and set by Britten in October 1937, the character of which we recognize immediately as having its roots in the thirties. But elsewhere *On this Island* breaks new ground in very interesting ways. 'Nocturne', for example—one of the best and most serious songs of the set—strikes an effortlessly lyrical note through its use of outwardly the simplest musical means, a rising and falling arpeggio, but one so subtly treated and developed that the simplicity is illusory: the song owes its impact to a complex web of imagery and feeling. I am sure Britten had this seeming simplicity in mind when he commented ironically on the reception of his songs at their first performance, 'too obvious & amenable for Contemporary music'. It is my guess that the audience, having succeeded in recognizing an arpeggio (see Ex. 11a) would have concluded that the music was not worth their attention and withdrawn their ears.

Ex. 11a

'Nocturne' is one of Britten's characteristic night pieces. The rising and falling arpeggio, out of which the whole song is built, encapsulates one of the principal images of the poem: a sleeper, a dreamer, the gentle rise and fall of his breathing, a sleeper about *to wake*; and the transition from sleep into consciousness generates a striking modification of the arpeggio's octave pattern on its final sung appearance in its ascending form—'Calmly till the morning break, let him lie'—and what Peter Evans has described as 'the most transfiguring modulation in the whole work':[20]

Ex. 11b

That radical change of state, from dreaming to wakefulness, also explains why for the final descending form of the arpeggio, the singer is silent and the piano takes over: wakefulness has taken over from slumber, dawn from night.

Now through night's caressing grip
Earth and all her oceans slip,
Capes of China slide away
From her fingers into day
And the Americas incline
Coasts towards her shadow line.
Now the ragged vagrants creep
Into crooked holes to sleep:
Just and unjust, worst and best,
Change their places as they rest:
Awkward lovers lie in fields
Where disdainful beauty yields:
While the splendid and the proud
Naked stand before the crowd
And the losing gambler gains
And the beggar entertains:
May sleep's healing power extend
Through these hours to our friend.
Unpursued by hostile force,
Traction engine, bull or horse
Or revolting succubus:
Calmly till the morning break
Let him lie, then gently wake.

I said I would not go much into the substance of these songs, and I am conscious of breaking that undertaking. But having broken it, I must point to Britten's tactful management of three lines, the musicalization of which, in an otherwise very accessible lyric, must have posed a problem:

Unpursued by hostile force,
Traction engine, bull or horse
Or revolting succubus;

Britten's neat solution was a series of repeated low C's, half-sung, half-spoken. It is a discreet response to the challenge, neither an unworthy attempt to suppress the words, nor, with exaggerated idealism, does it set out actually to promote them.

There is much that might be said about these Auden settings, and especially about their forms in relation to the texts and the proliferation of musical ideas which might be thought not so much to match the poetic ideas or images but rather to embody them. In short, adumbrated in *On this Island* are many of the techniques that were to serve Britten throughout a creative life in which particular attention was to be paid to song, to the association of words and music in diverse forms and for diverse occasions, to the exploration of much poetry and its possibilities for music. Much of this was initiated in *On this Island*, just as much of Britten's own knowledge and experience of English poetry, of the resources of English words and the English language were immeasurably widened and deepened through his collaboration and friendship with Auden; and because *On this Island* marks the beginning of that penetrating musical exploration of English poetry, the song collection has a crucial importance in Britten's *oeuvre*.

I am aware, of course, that by 1937 Britten had already set many English words. As a child he had composed songs with texts by many different English poets, living and dead, and from about 1930 onwards there was a whole crop of works—mostly part-songs and works for chorus—using English texts; and then there were the songs and choruses written for the theatre, the cabaret songs and *Our Hunting Fathers*. So it would be absurd to suggest that Britten did not have a substantial experience of the musicalization of English words already behind him. However, there are, I think, important qualifications to be made. Writing for the theatre taught Britten a lot that was valuable, but the context inevitably imposed certain constraints: the music had to be kept pretty simple and draw largely on the vernacular for its style. And while not underestimating the compositional challenge Britten took on in certain of his early choral works — in *A Boy was Born*, for example, the texts of which comprised a miniature anthology of medieval English verse—choral setting and scoring represent an encounter between music and words of a quite different nature from that involved in solo song. As for *Our Hunting Fathers*, the song-cycle for voice and orchestra, I would be the last person to deny the power and audacious brilliance of the word-setting, the originality of which is one of the work's most conspicuous features. However, I think it has to be admitted that *Our Hunting Fathers* was a unique case and that its singular vocal writing was intimately bound up with the particular character and message, and the particular sound-world, of that work. It was not an approach to language that could be pressed into general service.

I would suggest that, when Britten's imagination was fired in 1936 by poems from Auden's *Look, Stranger!* volume, and while he was setting them throughout the following year, he was in some respects confronted for the first time with many of the problems that are bound up with the musicalization of a poem, a lyric, which in its own right is a self-contained, tightly organized form—already an ordered disposition of *verbal* sonorities. *On this Island* was not only Britten's first set of songs, if not a cycle then certainly a carefully considered collection, but it was also his first *major* confrontation with English verse as a song-writer, and one made through the medium of Auden's use of the English language. There can be no doubt that the energy and strangeness and freshness of Auden's English formed part of the appeal; the poems constituted a great challenge and Britten, interestingly, did not find the going all that easy. In particular, the first song 'Let the florid music praise!'[21] gave him endless trouble. His diary entry for 25 September 1937 gives us some idea of the difficulties he was facing:

> Up by mistake rather late, so I don't do all the work I want to. However—I have time to do about 6 versions of the beginning of 'Florid Music' one of W. H. A.'s songs & all of them N.B.G.—I have never had such a devil as this song.

The difficulties were ones that Britten had met before; and there is something very familiar about a remark in his diary four months earlier on 26 May, when he was first starting to struggle with 'Let the florid music praise!': 'middle is bad tho' beginning & end good'. These were difficulties that, given time, Britten's compositional skills might reasonably have been expected to solve, but the techniques currently available to him could not, even with persistent application, easily resolve the larger problem of the need to find a music that would not merely enhance, illustrate or accompany, but assimilate and embody the word, and finally disgorge the indissoluble mix of word-sounds and musical pitches that we call song.

Britten himself must have been aware of this need which also entailed finding a compositional method, creating a working relationship between words and music. There can be no doubt that the often dazzling music and brilliant imagery of Auden's verse made Britten's search the harder and the more necessary. There were no immediate precedents to help him. Contemporary song in England in the thirties was of no use to him as a model. As Peter Pears put it in 1952, 'Very few settings of contemporary poets will be found among the songs published [in the thirties]. We are still lying on Bredon Hill or rollicking it with Shakespeare's contemporaries.'[22] Nor had Britten discovered Purcell, as he was to, profoundly, later.

He had to start somewhere, and it is fascinating and revealing, I think, to look at what he made of the opening of 'Let the florid music praise!' Prompted no doubt by the instrumental references in the text and by Auden's specification of 'florid music', Britten locates his start by turning to the past, even to Handel. The energy with which the song begins is wholly Brittenesque; indeed, the exuberant vocal cadenza — exuberant rather than extravagant — is obviously indebted to the virtuoso vocal style of *Our Hunting Fathers*. But in the song the exuberance is contained, inescapably so, because the chosen style of the opening is itself contained within the frame of a past convention — more specifically the kind of gestures we associate with the Baroque:

Ex. 12

'Let the florid music praise!' is one of the very few examples of a serious neo-classicizing spirit in Britten, but the style admirably projects the ceremonial proclamation of the first verse, the public statement, while at the same time providing the composer with a platform from which to launch himself. However, it was the middle of the song that Britten had to wrestle with, precisely at the point where in the latter half of the text public statement gives way to private imagery and to quite another and more complex language:

> O but the unloved have had power,
>   The weeping and striking,
> Always; time will bring their hour:
> Their secretive children walk
> Through your vigilance of breath
> To unpardonable death,
>   And my vows break
>   Before his look.

The second verse was a challenge for Britten. Here, he could not summon the past—an established convention—to his aid but had to rely solely on his own powers of invention and imagination. It was immeasurably the more difficult task, not only to project private rather than public images but to make a unity of those public and private worlds. If Britten may be said to have succeeded, as I think he did, then his success derives from his solution of the formal problem. As Ex. 13 below shows, he secures his musical unity by unfolding in the second verse the simplest and yet most transfiguring of modifications of the musical materials (× in the examples) out of which the first, the public, section is built. The song's brilliance resides in that compositional process, which generates the most powerful contrasts and at the same time integrates them as two aspects of the same idea—'Private faces / In public places':

Ex. 13

Peter Pears was surely right to describe 'Let the florid music praise!' as 'a salutary challenge to a whole generation of English songs'.[23] It seems likely that it was among the songs that Wystan Auden heard on 17 June, before the set had been completed, probably in a play-through with Britten at the piano. There are few recorded comments of Auden on Britten's settings of his texts,[24] but we learn on this occasion from Britten's diary that 'Wystan is terribly pleased with my straight songs for Sophie'—'straight', in order to distinguish the *Look, Stranger!* settings from the cabaret songs Britten was concurrently writing for Hedli Anderson.

Part of the importance and fascination of *On this Island*—and Britten was still in his early twenties when he composed the songs — rests in the insights the work gives us into how a composer who was to become a master of English song tackled his first adult solo songs to English texts; insights into the problems he encountered and variously resolved; and into how he achieved his successes, of which 'Nocturne' is a conspicuous example, where it is Britten's own voice that sings throughout and a highly sophisticated formal relationship between the text and the music emerges. 'Nocturne' very clearly indicates the way his mind was to work in the future when writing songs.

On this Island was a momentous encounter with English poetry and perhaps that it happened at all—and undoubtedly that it happened in the way it did—we owe to Auden, as indeed we owe to him a further stage in the history and development of Britten as song-writer. Perhaps as a result of his awareness of the problems of setting English that he had only partially resolved, after *On this Island* Britten turned away from English to French, to *Les Illuminations*; and then to Italian, in the *Seven Sonnets of Michelangelo*. It was not until he had completed these explorations of other languages that he felt able to return to his own, with many of the earlier problems now solved. It was through Auden that Britten was introduced to Rimbaud, hence *Les Illuminations*; and there is a nice symmetry in the fact that one of the works in which Britten in the early forties re-established and re-affirmed what was now to be a virtually unceasing creative dialogue with the English language was the *Hymn to St Cecilia*, a choral setting of words by Auden and a work of notable inspiration and flawless technique.[25] (It was in fact Britten's last major setting of a text by his old friend, though the *Spring Symphony* of 1949 was to make use of part of Auden's 'Out on the lawn I lie in bed'.)[26]

Between 1937 and 1942, when the *Hymn* was completed, at sea, aboard ship, as Britten voyaged back to wartime England, leaving Auden behind him in the States, there were many notable projects on which the poet and the composer had worked together. Above all, within this period, as the thirties gave way to the forties, there was *Paul Bunyan*, the operetta for which Auden wrote the libretto, Britten's first full-length work for the musical theatre, first performed in New York in 1941. *Paul Bunyan* warrants a study in its own right: in my view it represents both a summation and a consummation of Britten's preceding collaborations with Auden in film, theatre and radio.

Throughout the years in the States, from 1939 to 1942, the friendship between Auden and Britten continued to be a close and fruitful one. Indeed, for a time, Britten, with Peter Pears, shared a home with Auden—the only time he was to do so—in an old brownstone in Brooklyn Heights; 7 Middagh Street. Auden was, as it were, housemaster, and among the other residents were Gypsy Rose Lee, Carson McCullers, Paul Bowles, Louis MacNeice and George Davis, the owner, who was later to marry Lotte Lenya, Kurt Weill's widow. There were many, many other colourful inhabitants and visitors. But although Denis de Rougemont, who visited the house in 1941, was left with the impression that 'all that was new in America in music, painting or choreography emanated from that house, the only center of thought and art that I found in any large city of the country', it was altogether too Bohemian for the two English musicians, Puritans both, who quitted Middagh Street after a few months, and left for the West Coast.[27]

If one were to compile a list of all the projects on which Britten and Auden collaborated between 1935 and 1942, I think the world would be astonished by its magnitude. It can be only ignorance of the extent of their collaboration that allows Clive James to write so confidently that 'unlike Brecht . . . Auden never met his Kurt Weill. He met [sic] Britten, but the results were meagre'.[28] The truth is that if one had to try to quantify the outputs of the two sets of collaborators, there would not be much between them in substance; and if anything, perhaps the balance would go in favour of Auden and Britten. If we added together all the Auden–Britten collaborations: films, theatre pieces and radio features; the major song-cycle for voice and orchestra, *Our Hunting Fathers*, and *Ballad of Heroes*; *Paul Bunyan*, a full-length work for the musical theatre, a very substantial piece of work despite the modest intentions of the authors; a duet, 'Underneath the abject willow'; a volume of songs, *On this Island*; numerous other songs not yet published or collected; and finally, the *Hymn to St Cecilia*, we should find that we have amassed a very large body of work which made a decisive contribution to the making of the thirties. The joint work of composer and poet constitutes part of the very sight and sound of the decade. Some parts of the joint *oeuvre* belonged more to the artists' private worlds; in others—*Our Hunting Fathers*, for example—private statement and public comment were combined, a manifestation of that phenomenon of 'Private faces / In public places' which in my opening lecture I singled out as a particular feature of the thirties, and which we have witnessed surfacing time and time again in the entries from Britten's diaries.

When one has completed scrutinizing in detail the achievements of the partnership, which I have only begun to do in these lectures, I believe one has to conclude that this was an exceptional case. We may fairly claim that there is nothing quite like it elsewhere in the history of the arts in the English-speaking world in this century: this interaction, this interplay, between a major poet and a major composer. Throughout the period of their friendship and collaboration, both were developing strongly as individuals, independently and together. Their association was not destined to continue, even intermittently: the calibre of their gifts and perhaps the size of their egos, were to drive them apart. It is as independent creators that we shall most often, and rightly, continue to think of them, but during the thirties and for a little while longer, it was otherwise. For what they accomplished then, when their names were so often joined in common cause and shared creativity, we should remember them, and salute them, together.

Soi Soonvichai, Bangkok; Ridgmount Gardens, London;
and Chapel House, Horham
August 1976—November 1979

Notes

1 *The English Auden*, p. 406.

2 In the GPO days, Basil Wright recalls that Auden dominated the scene and was a great talker; while Britten was very quiet and withdrawn. There is also much evidence from friends and observers of Auden's seeming compulsion to advise his friends about their mode of life, to assess their merits and their relationships (marital and other), and their futures; and also to lay out their failures (as he saw them) for inspection and correction. A fascinating example of this magisterial attitude has come to light at a late stage in the compilation of this version of the lectures and I am much indebted to two members of the Mayer family—Mrs Beata Sauerlander and the Reverend Michael Mayer—and to Professor Mendelson and his co-Executors of the Estate of W. H. Auden for generously facilitating the publication here of the following letter, which is in the possession of the Berg Collection of the New York Public Library (curator, Ms Lola Szladits). The letter, Professor Mendelson suggests, was probably written on 31 January 1942. Britten and Pears had clearly conveyed the news of their imminent return to the United Kingdom to Auden who— as we know from a hand-written entry in Elizabeth Mayer's 1941 calendar—had moved to Ann Arbor on 28 November. No doubt Britten's and Pears's friends would have expected them to leave more quickly than they actually succeeded in doing: it was not until 16 March 1942 that they left New York, to start their journey home. The last paragraph of the letter refers to Auden's *For the Time Being*, a Christmas Oratorio which was originally conceived as a text for setting by Britten. The project never materialized however, except for Britten's setting of the final Chorale (for a BBC feature programme, *A Poet's Christmas*, in 1944), and Auden published his complete poem in 1945.

Saturday   as from 1504 Brooklyn Avenue
                                   Ann Arbor (I move in Tuesday)

Dearest Ben,
Very guilty about not having written. Perhaps I can't make
myself believe that you are really leaving us. I need scarcely say,
my dear, how much I shall miss you and Peter, or how much I
love you both.

There is a lot I want to talk to you about, but I must try and say
a little of it by letter. I have been thinking a great deal about you
and your work during the past year. As you know I think you the
white hope of music; for this very reason I am more critical of you
than of anybody else, and I think I know something about the
dangers that beset you as a man and as an artist because they are
my own.

Goodness and [Beauty] are the results of a perfect balance
between Order and Chaos, Bohemianism and Bourgeois
Convention.

Bohemian chaos alone ends in a mad jumble of beautiful
scraps; Bourgeois convention alone ends in large unfeeling
corpses.

Every artist except the supreme masters has a bias one way or
the other. The best pair of opposites I can think of in music are
Wagner and Strauss. (Technical skill always comes from the
bourgeois side of one's nature.)

For middle-class Englishmen like you and me, the danger is
of course the second. Your attraction to thin-as-a-board
juveniles, ie to the sexless and innocent, is a symptom of this.
And I am certain too that it is your denial and evasion of the
demands of disorder that is responsible for your attacks of ill-
health, ie sickness is your substitute for the Bohemian.

Wherever you go you are and probably always will be
surrounded by people who adore you, nurse you, and praise
everything you do, eg Elisabeth, Peter (Please show this to P to
whom all this is also addressed). Up to a certain point this is fine

for you, but beware. You see, Bengy dear, you are always tempted to make things too easy for yourself in this way, ie to build yourself a warm nest of love (of course when you get it, you find it a little stifling) by playing the lovable talented little boy.

If you are really to develop to your full stature, you will have, I think, to suffer, and make others suffer, in ways which are totally strange to you at present, and against every conscious value that you have; ie you will have to be able to say what you never have had the right to say—God, I'm a shit.

This is all expressed very muddle-headedly, but try and not misunderstand it, and believe that it is only my love and admiration for you that makes me say it.

Here are one and a half more movements. The second half of the fourth movement will be about the Taxing of the People.

All my love to you both, and God bless you

Wystan

It seems to me that that letter requires no elaborate commentary. But I would wish to remark that while it shows, I think, the warmth of Auden's affection and the strength of his admiration—it was, I am sure, written as a *loving* letter—it also shows the difficulties inherent in the relationship. There was something exceptionally but perhaps characteristically *un*realistic about Auden's hope that his strictures, which leave as little room for debate as a Headmaster's final report, would not be misunderstood (especially when one bears in mind Britten's own abnormal sensitivities and anxieties, to which Auden can hardly have been blind). Possibly the most extraordinary aspect of the letter, for all that it illumines the difficulties of a complex relationship, resides in the earlier part where Auden dwells on the balance between 'Order and Chaos, Bohemianism and Bourgeois Convention' and the 'demands of disorder'. For what else is this but an unveiling of the very topic that was Britten's concern throughout his later creative life and formed the substance — the heart — of his last opera, *Death in Venice?* *

3 W. H. Auden, *Look, Stranger!* (London: Faber & Faber, 1936).

4 W. H. Auden, *Paul Bunyan*, Libretto, unpublished copy in the Berg Collection, New York Public Library, 1941, 1–2–20 (i.e. Act I, scene ii, p. 20). Verses 1, 3, 4 and 6 of 'Love Song' (No. 15 in the 1941 version) are quoted here. For the Johnny-Chorus dialogue, see 1–2–21 to 1–2–22 (i.e. Act I, scene ii, pp. 21–22).

5 See publisher's prefatory note in *Paul Bunyan*, Vocal Score, pp. ix–x.

6 In his later collaborations with Stravinsky and Henze, Auden would have encountered a very different approach to words—a wholly different set of demands—from Britten's.

7 This particular poem (*The English Auden*, p. 160) appears to address itself to a feature of the youthful Britten's character which was of concern to his friends: his reluctance (was it so?) to engage in warm, loving—presumably sexual—relationships. This is surely what the lyric implies, the final stanza of which is an invitation to Britten to abandon his posture. 'Strike', says Auden, 'and you shall conquer':

> Geese in flocks above you flying
>   Their direction know;
> Brooks beneath the thin ice flowing
>   To their oceans go;
> Coldest love will warm to action,
>   Walk then, come,
>   No longer numb,
> Into your satisfaction.

*A final note: Peter Pears, on re-reading this letter almost 40 years on, remarked that the particular psychologizing reflected not only a current enthusiasm of Auden's—Groddeck?—but also, more physically, the actual state of the house that he and Britten shared with the poet for some months in 1940–41 and from which they—the self-confessed representatives of Bourgeois Convention—were driven by the conditions of Bohemian chaos amid which Auden chose to live at 7 Middagh Street. Their retreat from the advantages of disorder may indeed have inspired at least part of this particular tirade.

Britten must have understood the message, of that there can be no question; but interestingly, the music as it were rejects the invitation. The composer maintains his distance and his reserve by his setting of the text as a brisk—jaunty, even—impersonal and highly mannered polka-like dance. As if that were not enough, the use of *two* voices virtually guarantees the keeping at arm's length of any intimation of a personal response on Britten's part. He could not have made it clearer that he declined to emerge as the song's protagonist, despite the text's dedication. The opening of the duet will suffice to indicate the distancing tone:

This complex aspect of Britten's personality as a young man was no doubt further reflected in, and reinforced by, his own feeling of being the youngest of the group, youngest in experience as well as years, to which I refer on p. 134. There is an incident related in *W. H. Auden, The Life of a Poet*, p. 128, which in its gossipy but enlightening way suggests that one of the reasons for Britten's reserve was his uncertainty about his own sexual nature. Perhaps he had to come to terms with himself before he could 'strike and conquer', as his friends wanted him to. For what it's worth, both the poems (very fine ones) dedicated to Britten in Auden's *Look, Stranger!* are conspicuously personal in voice; and the 'Lullaby' which Auden wrote into one of Britten's scores (see n. 8 below) became one of the poet's most famous love poems, and justly so.

8 The score remained in Britten's possession but was borrowed from him at some stage and never returned. The 'Lullaby' to which he refers in his diary entry was 'Lay your sleeping head, my love' (*The English Auden*, p. 207); and this was scribbled in pencil into the vocal score of *Our Hunting Fathers*, which Britten must have had with him on the same occasion. This score is preserved in the Britten-Pears Library at Aldeburgh. About the 'Lullaby', Professor Mendelson (*Early Auden*, Chapter 10, 'The Insufficient Touch') writes: 'A few days after writing [the poem] Auden left for Spain, moving from his divided private world to the divided public one. "Lullaby" was both the culminating statement of his emotional life up to now and an innovation in English poetry—the only serious poem in which a lover proclaims to the beloved, in moral terms and during a shared night of love, his own faithlessness.' Professor Mendelson also has interesting and enlightening things to say about Auden's decision to go to Spain.

9 See Arnold Rattenbury on Randall Swingler, quoted in *Reading the Thirties*, p. 8.

10 Benjamin Britten, *Ballad of Heroes*, Vocal Score (London: Boosey & Hawkes, 1939), pp. 1 and 37. At a late stage in the preparation of this book for publication, and some long while after the lectures themselves had been written and delivered, my attention was brought to the singular fact that the Scherzo of the *Ballad*

had its origin in some incidental music Britten had written for a BBC radio play, *King Arthur*, broadcast in April 1937, i.e. two years *before* the *Ballad* was composed and first performed. (I am much indebted to Dr Colin Matthews who spotted the connection. Incidentally, Britten was to plunder *King Arthur* yet again, when revising his piano concerto in 1945.) It is out of No. XIVA of the *King Arthur* score, the first page of which number is reproduced in *Benjamin Britten 1913-1976: Pictures from a Life*, ill. 104, that the Scherzo of the *Ballad* was to emerge:

Ostinato of *King Arthur* and *Ballad of Heroes*

A comparison of the two scores shows that Britten substantially remodelled and expanded the purely instrumental *King Arthur* number when conscripting it for use in the choral and orchestral Scherzo of the *Ballad*. The Scherzo runs to 191 bars, No. XIVA to 110 bars (which include a repeated section of 40 bars which is not a feature of the Scherzo). Moreover, while Britten does not fail to use most of the principal ideas from his 'wild dance' of 1937 in the Scherzo of 1939—and in particular it is the fierce, rotating ostinato that is the common concept uniting the two movements— the entire molto pesante passage in the *Ballad*, with the dramatic trumpet fanfares (from the gallery) which so unmistakably antici- pate comparable gestures from the *War Requiem*, is new. Thus it is more accurate to think of this revival of No. XIVA from *King Arthur* in the *Ballad of Heroes* as re-composition rather than revision or re-arrangement.

The number in question was heard as the script's so-called 'Thirteenth Link' came to its end; and was associated with Lancelot's attempt to control 'the company of the Round Table':

> For some are jealous of his old renown,
> And some are angry at the love he bears
> For Guenevere the Queen, and envy spares
> No censure that can drag his honour down.
>
> And like the bodings of a direful storm
> The growl of rumour gathers to a head. . . .

At the end of this passage 'A riotous and rather terrifying dance is faded up sharply', which then provides 'a quiet background' for the scene that follows: 'Scene 13: The Queen Betrayed', in which the jealousies, intrigues and disaffections of the Court boil up to a climax. Here, we read in the script, 'The music surges in again, whirls on, and after making its suggestion of the letting loose of every demon in hell fades slowly down to silence. . . .'

It seems worth spelling out the details of the dramatic context in which the Scherzo first appeared because it explains why the music must have returned to Britten's mind in 1939 when putting together the *Ballad of Heroes*. The 'letting loose of every demon in hell' that accompanied a dramatic peak in Scene 13 of *King Arthur* must have seemed peculiarly relevant to the political situation in 1939, with its piling-up overtones of war, the growing sense of demons waiting to be unleashed; and indeed it is the chief demon of all who stalks through Auden's verses:

> For the Devil has broken parole and arisen,
> He has dynamited his way out of prison,
> Out of the well where his Papa throws
> The rebel angel, the outcast rose.

Britten was ever consistent in his imagery and the 'demonic' link between *King Arthur* and the *Ballad* brings further confirmation of an habitual trait. It was not only a matter of economy of time, labour and materials, though it was clearly that too.

The substantial score of *King Arthur* was sketched and orchestrated between 19 March and 19 April 1937. On the 20th the rehearsals began, and the drama was broadcast by the BBC, on the

National wavelength, on the evening of the 23rd, when the orchestra was conducted by Clarence Raybould. The script was by D. G. Bridson and the producer was Val Gielgud. Britten did not much enjoy the commission if his diary entries are anything to go by—'It's a curse having to go on & on with this awful bore of Uncle Arthur', he wrote on 11 April; and the final rehearsal and performance on the 23rd did not do much to modify his dissatisfaction with the venture:

> Early to the BBC. at 10.15 for full rehearsal — it goes quite well, apart from a few misunderstandings—tho' the actual play irritates me more than I can say—its stilted dialogue, a pale pastiche of Malory—its dull Tennysonian poetry, & not nearly as good as that either—& its complete divorce from realities or humanities. . . .

> Back to BBC for the King Arthur show — at 7.30. It goes very well — but I still feel the same about it. The music certainly comes off like hell & the orchestra & Lennox Berkeley (who comes with me, & with whom I eat at Café Royal after) was enthusiastic about it.

However, the Scherzo was clearly worth saving and we must be grateful to the *Ballad* for effecting its rescue. 'Uncle Arthur' was not all loss.

11 *The English Auden*, p. xix.
12 *The English Auden*, p. 208.
13 Ralph Fox was an English Marxist critic of the thirties and author of *The Novel and the People*. For an assessment of Fox and his work, see *The Auden Generation*, pp. 256–7.
14 *Look, Stranger!* was a title wished on the volume by Auden's publishers (Faber & Faber) without his consent. The USA edition was issued as *On this Island*, which he preferred. Hence, no doubt, Britten's adoption of that title for his volume of songs.
15 'Now through night's caressing grip', *The English Auden*, p. 283.
16 'O the valley in the summer where I and my John', *The English Auden*, p. 213.
17 Some further settings of Auden were actually done but have remained unpublished. Basil Wright, in an interview recorded for

the BBC (his interlocutor was Anthony Friese-Greene), remembered that the setting of 'Look, stranger, on this island now', i.e. 'Seascape' from *On this Island*, was originally done for a travel film that was never made. This, however, seems to be a not quite accurate recollection. Professor Mendelson writes (in a private communication): '"Seascape" was fairly definitely done for a travel film, not made by the GPO, but by Marion Grierson on behalf of the Travel and Industrial Association of Great Britain and Ireland . . . . The film was called *Beside the Seaside*, and, as finally made, included only a few phrases from the poem, not the poem itself.' Thus it is clear, I think, that while there was a textual relation between the film and Auden's poem, Britten's setting of 'Seascape' was independent of the film, as indeed the date of its composition —recorded in Britten's diary for 1937 (12 October)—would suggest. The film was made by the same company—Strand Films —that was later to be involved in the making of *Peace of Britain* and *The Way to the Sea*. See also *W. H. Auden, A Bibliography, 1924–1969*, p. 257.

18 Benjamin Britten, *On this Island* (London: Boosey & Hawkes, 1938).
19 *The English Auden*, p. 163.
20 Peter Evans, *The Music of Benjamin Britten* (London: Dent, 1979), p. 75.
21 *The English Auden*, p. 158.
22 Peter Pears, 'The Vocal Music' in *Benjamin Britten, A Commentary on his works*, p. 65.
23 *Benjamin Britten, A Commentary on his works*, p. 63.
24 However, in his unpublished tribute to Britten on the occasion of his 50th birthday, Auden wrote: 'What immediately struck me, as someone whose medium was language, about Britten the composer, was his extraordinary musical sensibility in relation to the English language. One had always been told that English was an impossible tongue to set or to sing. Since I already knew the songs of the Elizabethan composers like Dowland (I don't think I knew Purcell then), I knew this to be false, but the influence of that great composer, Handel, on the setting of English had been

unfortunate. There was Sullivan's settings of Gilbert's light verse to be sure, but his music seemed so boring. Here at last was a composer who could both set the language without undue distortion of its rhythmical values, and at the same time write music to which it was a real pleasure to listen.' Further, in *The Dyer's Hand* (London: Faber & Faber, 1963) in the essay 'Notes on Music and Opera', p. 433, Auden writes: 'There have been several composers, Campion, Hugo Wolf, Benjamin Britten, for example, whose musical imagination has been stimulated by poetry of a high order.' This must be one of the very few published references to Britten made by Auden in the post-war years, if not indeed the only one. See also Bryan Kelly, 'W. H. Auden, a musical guest' in the *Royal College of Music Magazine*, Vol. 76, No. 1, London, 1980, pp. 15–9, and especially p. 18.

25 The other works included the *Serenade*, for tenor, horn and strings, *Rejoice in the Lamb*, *A Ceremony of Carols* and *Peter Grimes*.

26 'Out on the lawn I lie in bed' (*The English Auden*, p. 136) was published in Auden's *Look, Stranger!* volume of 1936, so it was a poem Britten would have known for many years. Professor Mendelson (*Early Auden*, Chapter 8, 'Lucky this Point') points out that the poem belongs to the period in 1933 when Auden was teaching at the Downs School (see also pp. 105–10) and adds the detail that 'he lies in bed out on the lawn—as did much of the school during that warm season. (When it rained he put up an umbrella over his head and went back to sleep.)'

27 See Virginia Spencer Carr, *The Lonely Hunter: A Biography of Carson McCullers* (New York: Doubleday, 1975) and especially 'Middagh Street, A Queer Menage', pp. 117–40; for the quotation from de Rougemont, see pp. 124–5. See also W. H. Auden, *The Life of a Poet*, pp. 196–8.

28 Clive James, *At the Pillars of Hercules* (London: Faber & Faber, 1979), p. 35.

Index

Agamemnon, The (Aeschylus, trans. MacNeice), 129

Anderson, Hedli, 107–8, 111, 128, 145, 156

Arundell, Denis, 127

Attlee, Clement, 22

Auden, Wystan Hugh, on art and politics, 25, 133–4; China, visit to, 111, 129; memorial service, 15; on pacifism, 96; school, 104; Spain, visit to, 105, 133, 141, 145, 165; 'As it is, plenty', 146–8; Ascent of F6, The (Auden-Isherwood), 31, 97–8, 118–24, 129, 130, 140, 145; Dance of Death, The, 48, 143; Dog Beneath the Skin, The (Auden-Isherwood), 87–8, 119–20, 122, 145; Dyer's Hand, The, 170; Elder Edda, The, 126; For the Time Being, 160; Hymn to St Cecilia, 15, 158; 'It's farewell to the drawing-room's civilised cry', 141–4, quoted, 167; 'Lay your sleeping head, my love', 165; 'Let the florid music praise!', 152–6; 'Letter to Lord Byron', 88; Look, Stranger!, 135, 140, 145, 152, 156, 165, 168; 'Look, stranger, on this island now', 168–9; Night Mail, end commentary, 80–5; 'Now through night's caressing grip', 148–50; 'O the valley in the summer where I and my John', 145; On the Frontier (Auden-Isherwood), 118; Orators, The, 24, 50, 129; Our Hunting Fathers, choice of texts, 32–4, Prologue, 48, 54–5, 135, Epilogue, 48–9, 54–5, 135; 'Out on the lawn I lie in bed', 157, 170; Oxford Poetry (Preface), 24; Paid on Both Sides, 103, 129; Paul Bunyan, 33, 136–9, 157, 158, text of original version, 136–7, 138; Poet's Tongue, The (Introduction), 25; 'Psychology and Art To-day', quoted, 25; Secondary Worlds, 125; 'September 1, 1939', 21–2; 'Sir, no man's enemy, forgiving all', quoted, 25; 'Tell me the truth about love', 128–9, 136; 'Underneath the abject willow', 140, 158, 163–5; Way to the Sea, The, 88–9, end commentary, 90–3. See also: Beside the Seaside, Calendar of the Year, Coal Face, God's Chillun, Poet's Christmas, A, Up the garden path

Aufstieg und Fall der Stadt Mahagonny (Brecht-Weill), 120

Baldwin, Stanley, 73

Barton, Francis, 28, 52

BBC, 29, 79–80, 105, 127, 146, 160, 165, 167–8

BBC News, 66

Berkeley, Lennox, 146, 168

Beside the Seaside (film), 169

Blake, William, 115, 129; 'The Little Black Boy' (Songs of Innocence), 129

Blunt, Anthony, 51–2

Boosey & Hawkes, 28, 70, 81

Boult, Adrian, 19

Bowles, Paul, 157

Boys, Henry, 28, 52

Brecht, Bertolt, 67, 71, 78, 96, 109, 120; Aufstieg und Fall der Stadt

Mahagonny (Brecht-Weill), 120;
Dreigroschenoper, Die (Brecht-
Weill), 120; *Massnahme, Die*
(Brecht-Eisler), 70–1, 96
Bridge, Ethel, 28, 52, 87, 98
Bridge, Frank, 28, 31, 32, 52, 87,
98, 100; Piano Trio No. 2, 77, 100
Bridson, D. G., 168; *King Arthur,*
165–8
Britten, Barbara, 77
Britten, Benjamin, childhood,
115–7; consistency of imagery,
37, 95, 142, 165–8; diaries, 13,
22–3, 27–8, 33, 45, 57, 59, 63,
76, 78, 119, ills., 18, 56, 102, 132;
quotations from, 13, 19, 28, 29,
31, 32, 34–5, 39, 41, 45, 46, 49,
57, 64, 65, 66, 67, 70–1, 73, 76,
77, 78, 79, 80–1, 83, 84–5, 87,
88, 97, 98, 107–8, 112, 113–4,
119–20, 124, 127, 128, 129, 133,
140, 141, 145, 146, 148, 152,
156, 167–8; music for young
people, 116–7; pacifism, 63, 67–
76; parody, 89; relationship with
Auden, 15, 133–6, 139–41,
157–9, 160–2, 163–5; school,
112–3; settings of T. S. Eliot, 13;
sound effects, 85–6; vocal writing
and word setting, 43–4, 151–3,
169–70; *Ballad of Heroes,* 142–4,
158, 165–8; *Billy Budd,* 116; *Boy
was Born, A,* 151; *Canticle IV:
Journey of the Magi,* 13; *Ceremony
of Carols, A,* 170; Church
Parables, 25; *Death in Venice,* 24,
37, 86, 163; *F6 Blues,* 108, 111,
122–4, 127, MS ill., 123; *Four
Cabaret Songs,* 95, 127, 156, 'Tell
me the truth about love', 109–
11, 117, 128–9, 136, 'Funeral
Blues' ('Stop all the clocks'), 108,
111, 'Johnny', 145, 'Calypso', 95;
Friday Afternoons, 117, 'There
was a Monkey', 117; 'Home Sweet
Home', variations on, 107, 112;

Hymn to St Cecilia, 15, 157, 158;
Illuminations, Les, 156; *Little
Sweep, The* (from *Let's Make an
Opera*), 116; *On this Island,* 145–
56, 158, 'Let the florid music
praise!', 152–6, 'Seascape',
168–9, 'Nocturne', 145, 148–51,
156, 'As it is, plenty', 146–8; *Our
Hunting Fathers,* 19–20, 22,
29, 31–49, 135, 142, 146, 151,
152, 153, 158, 165; political
symbolism, 34–5, 43, 47–8, 54,
programme notes (by Britten), 53,
54, Prologue, 48, 54, 135, 'Rats
Away!', 34–42, 44, 46, 48, 95,
MS ill., 40, 'Messalina', 34,
39–42, 'Dance of Death', 39–48,
confusion between hawks and
hounds, 43, 53–4, Epilogue,
48–9, 54–5, 135; *Owen
Wingrave,* 116, *Pacifist March,*
67, ill., 68–9; *Paul Bunyan,* 33,
130, 136–9, 157, 158; *Peter
Grimes,* 30, 76, 170; Piano
Concerto (revised version), 165;
Rape of Lucretia, The, 67; *Rejoice
in the Lamb,* 170; *Russian
Funeral,* 70–8, 95, 97, MS ill.,
74–5; *Saint Nicolas,* 116;
Serenade, 170; *Seven Sonnets of
Michelangelo,* 156; *Sinfonia da
Requiem,* 143; *Sinfonietta,* 22,
141; *Soirées Musicales,* 81; *Spring
Symphony,* 157; *Turn of the
Screw, The,* 116; 'Underneath the
abject willow', 140, 158, 163–4;
*Variations on a Theme of Frank
Bridge,* 89; 'War and Death', see
Russian Funeral; War Requiem,
67, 133, 142, 166; 'Wind Song'
(*Stay down miner*), 100; *Winter
Words,* 95, 'Midnight on the Great
Western', 95. See also: *Beside the
Seaside, Coal Face, God's
Chillun, King Arthur, King's
Stamp, The, Night Mail, Pageant*

*of Empire, Poet's Christmas, A,
Timon of Athens, Up the garden
path, Way to the Sea, The*
Britten, Beth (Mrs C. E. Welford),
28, 29, 52(n. 18), 81, 98, 119
Britten, Mrs (Britten's Mother), 39,
77–8
Britten, Robert, 29, 52(n. 19), 105,
107, 117
Burhop, Eric, 51–2
Bush, Alan, 70–1, 96, 97
Bush, Nancy, 96

Cadbury, George, 63
Calendar of the Year (film), 81,
100(n. 25)
Campion, Thomas, 170
Cavalcanti, Alberto, 28, 57, 80–1,
94
Chamberlain, Neville, 52
Cheatle, John, 105–7, 127
Christian Science, 78, 100
Clark, Edward, 94
Clinton-Baddeley, V. C., 127
Clurman, Harold, 130
Coal Face (film), 83, 85, 94
Coldstream, William, 28, 86–7,
107–8
Columbia Theater Associates, 130
Communist Party of Great Britain,
25–7
Connolly, Cyril, 112–3; *Enemies of
Promise*, quoted, 113
Crawford, Cheryl, 130
Cripps, Stafford, 63–4

Daily Herald, 66
Daily Telegraph, 126
Daily Worker, 26, 142
Dart, Vera, 98
Davis, George, 157
de la Mare, Walter, 116
de Rougemont, Denis, 157
Doone, Rupert, 71, 87, 96, 97–8,
111, 118–20, 128, 129–30, 134
Dowland, John, 169

Downs School, The, 105–8,
111–2, 117, 122
Dreigroschenoper, Die, (Brecht-
Weill), 120
Dukes, Ashley, 121, 130
Duncan, Ronald, 67; *Pacifist
March*, 67, ill., 68–9; *Rape of
Lucretia, The*, 67
Dunkeley, Piers, 28, 52

Eddy, Mary Baker, 78, 100; *Science
and Health, Key to the Scriptures*,
100
Edward VIII, 78
Eisler, Hanns, 67, 70–1, 78, 96;
Massnahme, Die (Brecht-Eisler),
70–1, 96
Elgar, Edward, 114
Eliot, Thomas Stearns, 13–4, 60,
118, 131; 'Journey of the Magi',
13; *Murder in the Cathedral*, 13;
Sweeney Agonistes, 118
Enemies of Promise (Connolly),
quoted, 113
Evans, Peter, 149
Expedient, The, see *Massnahme, Die*
Exhumations (Isherwood), quoted,
103

Faber & Faber, 60
Faber, Geoffrey, 60
Façade (Walton), 120
Farewell to Arms, A, (Hemingway),
73
Fascism, 34–5, in Spain, 46, 145
Finney, Brian, 122
Fox, Ralph, 145, 168
Fuller, John, 48

Garrett, John, 25
Gielgud, Val, 168
Gilbert, William Schwenk, 170
Gisli the Outlaw, 103, 125
God's Chillun (film), 129
GPO Film Unit, 28, 29, 57, 58, 59,

62–5, 79, 80–8, 94, 100–1, 107, 160, 169

Gresham's School, Holt, 104
Grierson, John, 28, 57, 59–60, 61, 62, 63, 80, 86, 94, 101
Grierson, Marion, 63, 169
Group Theatre (London), 29, 48, 59, 71, 87, 118–24, 129–30, 143, 145
Group Theatre (USA), 130

Handel, Georg Frideric, 153, 169
Hardy, Thomas, 'Midnight on the Great Western', 95
Harvey, Trevor, 85
Hawkes, Ralph, 81, 128
Hemingway, Ernest, Farewell to Arms, A, 73
Henze, Hans Werner, 163
Hitler, Adolf, 45, 52, 79
Holzmann, Rudolph, 79
Howard, Brian, 107
Hynes, Samuel, 20, 23, 24, 25, 27, 103

Isherwood, Christopher, 31, 71, 96, 100, 103–4, 111, 118, 127–8, 134, 142, 146, pacifism, 96; Exhumations, quoted, 103, Memorial, The, 100; Ascent of F6, The, Dog Beneath the Skin, The, On the Frontier (Auden-Isherwood), see Auden
Italian-Abyssinian War, 34–5, 45, 73, 76

Jackson, Pat, 85
Jacob, Gordon, quoted, 36, 53
James, Clive, 158

King Arthur (Bridson), 165–8
King's Stamp, The, (film), 94
Kipling, Rudyard, 104, 126
Korchinska, Maria, 84

Labour Party, 26

Lambert, Constant, 142
Layton, David, 98
League of Nations, 64, 78, 79, 95
League of Nations Union, 63–4, 95
Lee, Gypsy Rose, 157
Left Review, 26
Left Revue, 29, 97–8
Left Theatre, 77, 100, 118
Legg, Stuart, 81, 84
Lehmann, John, 128
Leigh, Charlotte, 127
Lenya, Lotte, 157
Lied von der Erde, Das (Mahler), 44–5
Listener, 101
Lloyd, Harold, 77
London Labour Choral Union, 70, 78, 96

McCullers, Carson, 157
MacNeice, Louis, 107, 118, 129, 130, 157; Agamemnon, The (trans.), 129; Out of the Picture, 118, 130
Mahler, Gustav, 31, 44–5, 49, 73; Lied von der Erde, Das, 44–5
Manchester Guardian, 66, 94
Marx, Karl, 46
Marxism, 51–2
Massnahme, Die (Brecht-Eisler), 70–1, 96
Memorial, The (Isherwood), 100
Mendelson, Edward, 14–5, 50, 51(n. 14), 54–5, 100–1, 126, 128–9, 142–3, 160, 165, 168–9, 170
Middagh Street, 7; Brooklyn Heights, 157, 163
Murder in the Cathedral (Eliot), 13
Murrill, Herbert, 119–20, 122
'Music for the People' Festival 1937, 142
Mussolini, Benito, 35, 45, 73

National Government, 26, 45
Nazism, 43, 51–2, 78

New Statesman, 45
News Chronicle, 66
Night Mail (film), 27, 28–9, 64–5,
  77, 80–5, 89, 100, 119, MS ill., 82
Norfolk and Norwich Triennial
  Musical Festival 1936, 19, 32,
  38–9, 49, 53(n. 28)

Out of the Picture (MacNeice), 118,
  130
Oxford Union 'King and Country'
  Resolution, 51

Pageant of Empire (Slater), 97–9
'Peace Film', The, see Peace of
  Britain
Peace of Britain (film), 16, 60, 63–7,
  88, 94–5, 169
Peace Pledge Union, 67, 95
Pears, Peter, 140, 143, 146, 157,
  160–3; on English song, 153; on
  'Dance of Death' (Our Hunting
  Fathers), 43; on 'Let the florid
  music praise!' (On this Island),
  156; on relationship between
  Britten and Auden, 15
Poet's Christmas, A (radio feature),
  160
Porter, Cole, 109
Pritt, D. N., 63
Pudney, John, 128
Purcell, Henry, 153, 169

Rabinovich, D., quoted, 73
Radio Times, 45
Ravenscroft, Thomas, 'Hawking for
  the Partridge', 32, 47, 53–4
Raybould, Clarence, 168
Reeve, Basil, 28, 52, 87
Richards, Bernard, 77, 100
Richards, Irene, 77, 100
Rimbaud, Arthur, Illuminations,
  Les, 156
Rotha, Paul, 16, 57–8, 60–1, 62,
  63–7, 88–9, 94–5, 101, 140
Royal College of Music, 53, 94

Science and Health, Key to the
  Scriptures (Eddy), 100
Shostakovich, Dmitri, 71–3, 97;
  Piano Concerto No. 1, 71, 97;
  Symphony No. 11, 72
Slater, Enid, 98
Slater, Montagu, 76, 97–100;
  Pageant of Empire, 97–9; Stay
  down miner, 76, 78, 100
South Lodge School, Lowestoft, 112
Spanish Civil War, 46, 72, 133, 141,
  142, 145
Speaight, Robert, 13, 119
Spender, Humphrey, 128
Spender, Stephen, 96, 118, 128
Stay down miner (Slater), 76, 78, 100
Strand Films, 63, 88, 101, 133, 169
Strasberg, Lee, 130
Strauss, Richard, 161
Stravinsky, Igor, 136, 163
Sullivan, Arthur, 170
Sweeney Agonistes (Eliot), 118
Swingler, Randall, 142

Taylor, J. J., 64
Times, The, 36, 51–2
Timon of Athens (Shakespeare), 129
Transport and General Workers'
  Union, 64
Trevelyan, Julian, 128
TUC, 63–4

Unity Theatre, 118
Up the garden path (radio broadcast),
  105–7, 126–7, programme as
  broadcast billing, 106
Varèse, Edgard, 83
Vaughan Williams, Ralph, 36, 114

Wagner, Richard, 161
Walton, William, 113–4, 120, 146;
  Façade, 120
Watt, Harry, 29, 81
Way to the Sea, The, (film), 16,
  88–9, 101, 133, 140, 169, end
  commentary, 90–3

Weelkes, Thomas, 42
Weill, Kurt, 71, 109, 120, 130, 157,
  158; *Aufstieg und Fall der Stadt
  Mahagonny* (Brecht-Weill), 120;
  Dreigroschenoper, Die (Brecht-
  Weill), 120
Welford, Mrs C. E., see Britten,
  Beth

Williams, Grace, 98
Wolf, Hugo, 170
Wright, Basil, 28, 64–5, 80–1, 87,
  160, 168
Wyss, Sophie, 19, 32, 145–6, 156